PSYCHOLOGY AND COMMON SENSE

PSYCHOLOGY AND COMMON SENSE

R. B. Joynson

Department of Psychology
University of Nottingham

Routledge & Kegan Paul
London and Boston

First published in 1974
by Routledge & Kegan Paul Ltd
Broadway House, 68–74 Carter Lane,
London EC4V 5EL
and 9 Park Street, Boston, Mass., 02108, USA
Set in Monotype Baskerville
and printed in Great Britain by
Ebenezer Baylis & Son Ltd
The Trinity Press
Worcester, and London

ISBN 0 7100 7827 7 (c)

ISBN 0 7100 7899 4 (p)

Library of Congress Catalog Card No. 73-92985

'To a deplorable degree, the obvious has disappeared from learned psychology, so that we have to rediscover it.'

Wolfgang Kohler

CONTENTS

PREFACE

When I began to study psychology, in the immediate post-war years at Oxford, there was a strong and widely held conviction that it should be treated as a natural science. This standpoint favoured the study of physiology and animal behaviour, and was most clearly expressed in the doctrine of behaviourism. The simpler forms of human behaviour were also admitted, if they were amenable to experimental study; but the more complex questions of human personality and social interaction were often dismissed as still outside the scope of scientific inquiry, nor could psychology offer much help at present in the solution of many practical problems. The foundations of a biological science must be firmly laid, before the superstructure of human psychology could be securely built.

If I have gradually come to be more impressed by the limitations of this outlook, than by its achievements, it is largely through cumulative experience. I reluctantly discovered that the experimental method, when applied even to the simpler human capacities, encounters difficulties which seem to me to be still generally under-estimated. I also found as a teacher that it offers too narrow a foundation, either for approaching the more important questions about human nature, or for providing the student with a realistic preparation for eventual professional work. Lastly I was fortunate to meet, in the late Professor W. J. H. Sprott at Nottingham, a distinguished representative of a broader approach to the problems of psychology.

When I tried to formulate these misgivings more clearly, I found that others were already engaged in the same task. During the last few years, sceptical criticism has been more widespread than for a long period; and a vigorous debate is in progress about the fundamentals of psychology and the form which it should take in the future. There is, I think, a good reason why this debate should have come at this time. The mainstream of scientific psychology has always believed that the study of the simpler forms of behaviour would one day provide the basis for an advance towards the more complex problems of human psychology. This was the ultimate objective. But this belief is now being put to the test. Over the past twenty years, psychologists have increasingly attempted to apply, to these more complex problems, the principles and methods which they have evolved mainly in the study of simpler behaviour. This movement is encountering, however, two forms of opposition. It has met the scepticism of a growing minority, who are equally concerned that these more difficult questions should be studied, but who prefer other methods and interpretations. It has also, less obviously, raised uneasy doubts among the more cautious exponents of biological science, who were by no means convinced that the time was yet ripe for these extensions.

This short book is a personal attempt to come to terms with our present doubts, and even more with our present certainties. It seems to me that the conventional assumptions of scientific psychology are breaking down, and that alternative possibilities must be considered. It is hardly necessary to add that the underlying problems are difficult in the extreme. They may be approached in many ways. I have chosen to begin with that knowledge of human nature which is given by ordinary good sense. I believe that this has been neglected by psychological science, and that we must pay attention to it if we are to do justice to our immense and elusive subject.

Certain parts of the argument have already been published in the *Bulletin of the British Psychological Society*, in two articles entitled 'The breakdown of modern psychology' (October 1970) and 'The return of mind' (January 1972).

I am especially grateful to my wife, who has always been a forthright critic of psychology.

1

THE LAYMAN'S UNDERSTANDING

In one of G. K. Chesterton's stories, a man dreams of emulating the great explorers. One day he sets sail from the West Country and heads out into the Atlantic, confident that he is destined to discover an unknown land. For many weeks he wanders across the ocean, buffeted by storms and uncertain of his position. At last, a coastline comes in view; and, as he approaches, he sees the towers and domes and minarets of a strange civilization. Greatly excited, he makes his way ashore. To his astonishment, the natives speak English. He has landed at Brighton.

The psychologists have dreamed of emulating the great natural scientists. They have noted the prodigious progress of experiment, from physics to physiology, and they have argued that the same methods should next be applied to human behaviour. We still know little more of human nature, they say, than once we knew of the solar system or the evolution of life. But the methods which have been so successful there can be equally successful here: we can attain the same powers of prediction and control over human behaviour that we have acquired over the world around us. Today, they are bearing down upon us. In earlier times, they claim, the ignorance of human behaviour was relatively unimportant. But now life is increasingly complex; problems of over-population, of economic and political unrest, become daily harder to resolve, and a technology of behaviour has become an urgent necessity. Fortunately, however, the science of human behaviour is at hand.

A disillusionment awaits them. Human nature is not an unknown country, a *terra incognita* on the map of knowledge. It is our home ground. Human beings are not, like the objects of natural science, things which do not understand themselves; and we can already predict and control our behaviour to a remarkable extent ourselves. Even people who are not psychologists understand each other very well. We speak English. The psychologists are landing at Brighton.

The ability which we all have, to understand ourselves and others, presents the psychologist with a paradoxical task. What kind of understanding does he seek, of a creature which already understands itself? The psychologist has often reacted to this problem by ignoring it, or by denying that the layman's understanding need be taken seriously. But the consequences of this reaction are disastrous, and sooner or later the psychologist must face the challenge.

Psychologists were reminded of this problem many years ago by Kohler, who referred to what he called 'the layman's conviction': 'The layman believes that he often feels directly why he wants to do certain things in a first situation, and certain other things in a second' (Kohler, 1947, p. 320). Kohler illustrated his point with what he called some 'obvious and almost commonplace observations' (ibid., pp. 323ff). When something which we have carefully arranged is disturbed, we know that our anger is provoked by this disturbance, and the anger is felt to be natural under the circumstances. At a concert, it is unquestionably the voice of the singer which arouses our admiration, not our neighbour's nose or the conductor's back or a hundred other things which are also present to our senses. On a hot day, our enjoyment derives from the cool drink before us, not from the chair over there or the spider on the wall. Kohler concluded that, if the layman is right, 'the forces which principally determine his mental trends and his actions are for the most part directly given in his experience' (ibid., p. 320).

It was deplorable, Kohler continued, that psychologists should so often overlook these commonplace facts, preferring alternative explanations which ignored the layman's insight. Psychologists believe that people do one thing rather than another because certain nerve paths are more permeable than others, or because they have acquired certain habits, or because they have certain unconscious motivations. Such explanations might sometimes be appropriate, for the layman does not always have insight; but this does not justify the prevalent neglect of the layman's conviction, or invalidate it when it occurs. Kohler (op. cit., p. 323) expressed his view of the importance of the layman's conviction as follows:

> The kind of experience which the layman claims to have plays hardly any explicit part in the scientific psychology of our time. I feel that I must take sides with the layman; that, for once, he rather than our science is aware of a fundamental truth. For the layman's conviction is likely to become a major issue in the psychology, neurology and philosophy of the future.

It seems to the writer that Kohler's words are as important today as when they were written; indeed, the deplorable effects of neglecting the layman's conviction have become even more evident with the passage of time.

The layman feels, most of the time, that he understands his own behaviour well enough. He almost always knows what he is doing and why he is doing it. He can tell us (if we need to be told) that he is painting his house to keep it smart and weather-proof; that he is buying a toy for his child's birthday; that he is digging the garden so that he can plant potatoes. We may judge that a man's motives are trivial, or immoral, or absurd; or we may suggest that he does not appreciate the consequences of his actions. But if we suggest that the layman's explanations are false, we imply that he is either a fool (he is digging his garden without knowing why), or a liar (he has deliberately misled us), or a hypocrite (he has misled himself). In practice, we assume that most people can achieve a certain minimum standard of self-knowledge and self-control, for if they do not, we regard them as needing special care and attention.

It is part and parcel of this ability which we all have, to

understand ourselves, that we also understand others. The understanding of self can hardly be separated from the understanding of others. To understand oneself involves understanding one's relations to others, and their relation to us. When I enter a shop, I expect the shopkeeper to want to sell, and he expects me to want to buy. Talking confirms this, and extends our mutual understanding. Everyday life is a vast network of such understandings, and most of the time it works very well. If it were not so, even the simplest social life would be impossible; and the complexity of civilized life reflects the remarkable extent to which human beings have proved capable of developing their mutual understanding.

At this point, the reader may urge that there is much that we do not know about human nature. This commonsensical understanding, it may be said, is often severely limited or highly unreliable; hence a scientific psychology is necessary and desirable. The premiss of this argument is certainly sound. Common sense is often wrong. But this by no means shows that we need a scientific psychology.

Certainly, one should not underestimate the frequent difficulties of understanding which arise. There are times in life, especially at adolescence, when we may be indecisive and filled with self-doubt, or when it is hard to gain self-control. Any important change in life is apt to leave us at a loss; and those who enjoy an easy temperament or a happy routine may be insensitive to the problems which others face. But these difficulties are often at least as much moral as intellectual, and they do not prove that we need the psychologist. With patience and good sense, much can be done. Unfortunately there are many occasions when more expert help is needed. Some people may prove to be mentally deficient or disordered, and so requiring special care. But such cases emphasize that most men, most of the time, are in their right minds and perfectly capable of handling their own affairs.

There are also limits – much more severe limits – to our understanding of others. We can rarely understand others as well as we understand ourselves, if only because the period of acquaintance is usually shorter, and invariably less exhaustive. No doubt there is much to learn from seeing ourselves as others see us. But it would be a great mistake to suppose that all others see one true picture of us, which differs from our own false view.

4

Probably different people see us in different ways, and our conception of ourselves, being gradually improved as we learn something from each, is not too wide of the mark. But our understanding of others clearly depends much on the period of acquaintance. A complete stranger evokes no more than wide and tentative expectations about human nature in general; though age, sex, and style of dress narrow the possibilities considerably. With longer acquaintance, understanding usually improves. We discover people's interests and note their abilities; we become familiar with their tastes and learn to bear with their quirks. If we are in doubt about their feelings or intentions, we can of course ask them; though we have to be careful, for so often it is none of our business. It is true that misunderstandings abound, but we usually know how to put them right, though we do not always want to do so. Since misunderstandings upset the ordinary course of life, we tend to exaggerate their frequency. In reality, the problem is frequently the reverse: not how to reach understanding, but how to avoid it. Our motives are usually so transparent that we sometimes have to go to great lengths to conceal them.

To refer to our everyday understanding is not, then, to imply that it is perfect. On the contrary, it may be extremely defective. It may be narrow and prejudiced, insensitive and cocksure. But these limitations by no means establish a need for psychology. The layman has more than his ordinary good sense to fall back on, if he wants to improve his understanding. Much of what is roughly called a humanist education is directed to this end. The historian and the biographer broaden our ideas about the range of human nature: when we study men who have lived under radically different circumstances from ourselves, or who have possessed qualities of character or intellect which are foreign to us, our standards of judgment are gradually transformed and improved. The playwright and the novelist achieve similar aims on the plane of imagination: their insights become embedded in the traditions of civilized life, and some at least of their sensitivity permeates society in general. Nor should we ignore those who believe that the historic religions can help us in the everyday business of living as well as in the crises of life.

Whatever its faults and limitations, the capacity of man to understand himself, and the capacity of men of varied genius to refine and extend that understanding, are among man's greatest and most remarkable characteristics. It may be possible to trace its simple beginnings among the higher animals, but nothing else of which we know in the universe bears comparison with man in this respect. If the psychologist did not exist, would it be necessary to invent him?

The argument does not establish that psychology can serve no good purpose. It does suggest, very strongly, that when the psychologist states his aims, he must consider with care what is the relation between the understanding which he seeks and that which we already have. He will not want to tell us what we knew before, nor will he want to deceive himself as well as us by disguising the familiar in pretentious jargon. His first step, we must expect, will be to draw our attention to this remarkable capacity of man, and warn us to be wary.

But psychologists, as Kohler complained, commonly adopt a very different attitude. They often write as if human nature was something which human beings have never come across. There are many introductory texts which do not mention our everyday understanding; others refer to it only to belittle it as unreliable guesswork. Especially among those psychologists who have been strongly influenced by the behaviourist tradition, we find that they write as if there was nothing whatever to be said in favour of ordinary good sense, and as if their own, allegedly scientific, information was the only ray of light in the darkness. Thus Skinner (1972, p. 160) writes: 'What, after all, have we to show for nonscientific or prescientific good judgment, or common sense, or the insights gained through personal experience? It is science or nothing.' Broadbent encourages the same attitude when he writes (1961, p. 200): 'The confident dogmatisms about human nature which fall so readily from pulpits, newspaper editorials, and school prizegivings are not for us.'

If this attitude was supported by a cogent examination of everyday understanding, it might be defensible. But the behaviourist is often, it seems to me, surprisingly superficial. Consider the following passage from Skinner (1972, pp. 12–13):

If we ask someone, 'Why did you go to the theater?' and he says, 'Because I felt like going,' we are apt to take his reply as a kind of explanation. It would be more to the point to know what has happened when he has gone to the theater in the past, what he heard or read about the play he went to see, and what other things in his past or present environments might have induced him to go (as opposed to doing something else), but we accept 'I felt like going' as a sort of summary of all this and are not likely to ask for details.

But surely, if we were given such a reply, we should take it, not as an explanation, but as a refusal of explanation. We should take it as a sign that the question was for some reason unwelcome, and of course we should not ask for details. And of course it would be more to the point to know all those things; but we do not need a psychologist to tell us – the person himself could do so if he wished.

The disparagement of ordinary good sense is frequently accompanied by a decidedly superior attitude towards humanist education. Broadbent dismisses the humanist tradition with a brief reference to an assumption, as he calls it, 'that the study of history or literature sheds more light on these spiritual problems than science does. This assumption tends to be unconvincing to scientists' (1961, p. 16). Skinner is even more sweeping. He lists political science, law, religion, economics, anthropology, sociology, psychotherapy, philosophy, ethics, history, education, child care, linguistics, architecture, city planning, and family life, and comments that there is 'a tremendous weight of traditional "knowledge", which must be corrected or displaced by a scientific analysis' (Skinner, 1972, p. 19).

Such writing implants in the student of psychology a foolish and dangerous bias. He is led to imagine that he will become one of a select band of scientific psychologists who will be able, for the first time in history, to provide proper explanations of human behaviour; as though nobody before had ever been able to think about it with rational detachment. In fact, he will learn either to underestimate, or entirely to overlook, the remarkable extent to which we already possess this capacity. Many psychologists seem determined to ignore the prime characteristic of their subject matter. Their blindness deserves a special name. The refusal to recognize our everyday understanding may be called 'the behaviourist's prejudice'.

We shall later ask how this prejudice arose, but first we may consider some of its consequences. It is easy for the psychologist to ignore the layman's conviction when he works out his theories in the seclusion of his laboratory. But he cannot then prevent the layman from forming his own impressions of the result. There are certain critical comments, which the layman frequently makes, which are highly relevant to the theme we have been following.

A programme was broadcast recently on television called 'The Child Experts'. Taking part were three psychologists, a psychiatrist, and a paediatrician, and they discussed the question how to bring up children. The next day the television critic of *The Times* (18 August 1969) reviewed the programme and made this comment: 'Somehow or other, it seemed that all the entirely reasonable things they said were things that any sensible person, especially any sensible parent, could easily work out for himself. One hopes that the less sensible ones were eagerly watching.' It might be suggested that the expert is bound to run into this difficulty sometimes, when he tries to give a popular account of his subject, and that of course it would have been possible to pitch the level higher. But did the experts realize that this was the impression they might give? It seems to me that this criticism is made far too often for the psychologist to accept such comforting explanations. Indeed, psychologists are thoroughly familiar with it. Argyle writes: 'It has been objected that the results of much social research are not surprising, that we knew them all before' (Humphrey and Argyle, 1962, p. 14). It is time to ask why this objection is made.

The psychologist's defence is usually as follows. If common sense is sometimes confirmed (he cautiously admits), this provides scientific grounds for accepting what was previously merely an intuitive guess. In any case (he quickly adds), common sense is not always confirmed. Thus Argyle, after noting the objection that results are sometimes 'not surprising', at once asserts that 'this is often not so' (ibid.). But it is altogether too easy to assume that, when the psychologist's conclusions run counter to common sense, it is the psychologist's conclusions which are correct and common sense which is wrong; and it is altogether too easy to assume that, when the psychologist's conclusions agree with common sense, what was previously only guessed has now been reliably established. These assumptions are not necessarily justified.

The layman's understanding, though often imperfect, is not

to be universally dismissed as intuitive guesswork, necessarily inferior to the special methods of the scientific psychologist. On the contrary, the layman's conclusions may well be based on long and varied experience, frequently interpreted, of course, by a highly trained intelligence. Experiment in psychology, by contrast, typically operates over short periods of time, in very restricted environments, and on narrow segments of behaviour. It would not be surprising if common sense often proved to be as reliable as experiment, and sometimes more reliable. So we should be prepared for the possibility that when the psychologist's conclusions differ from common sense, it is common sense which is correct; and also for the possibility that, when the psychologist's conclusions agree with common sense, it is the psychologist who has made the lucky guess.

Here is an example. In a widely used textbook of *Social Psychology*, Brown refers to what he calls a 'recent discovery' which 'goes counter to popular belief'. The discovery is that 'the decisions made by people in groups are riskier than the decisions which the same people make when they are in isolation from one another' (1965, p. xxiii). Thus Brown is claiming that the popular belief is that group decisions are *less* risky, whereas experiment shows that they are *more* risky. It is first necessary to determine whether there is such a popular belief, for if Brown is mistaken about this, he can hardly claim to have refuted it, even if the 'recent discovery' proves genuine. In order to investigate the popular opinion (and this phrase itself betrays a superior attitude to the layman's views), I put the following question to a first year class in social psychology, who were unfamiliar with the problem: 'Would you expect that decisions taken in groups would be more risky, less risky, or much the same, as decisions taken in isolation?'

It was soon obvious that in this group at least there was no readymade 'popular belief' at all. The question was treated as complex, and a general discussion ensued in which several further queries were raised: what was the decision? how much depended on its outcome? who were the people? did they know each other well? how long did they have to decide? and so on. After a few minutes, a consensus of opinion emerged. It was not sensible to expect any simple generalization to hold. The outcome must depend upon the interplay of a variety of factors, and sometimes the decision might be more risky, sometimes less

9

risky, and sometimes much the same. Our first conclusion, then, is that Brown failed to do justice to ordinary good sense. There does not seem to be a popular belief that group decisions will be *less* risky.

We may now consider the 'recent discovery' that group decisions are *more* risky. Brown states that this 'has proved difficult to explain', and spends some fifty pages attempting to do so. His conclusion may be gathered from the following extracts, which provide a lively picture of the psychologist in the throes of creative endeavour (Brown, 1965, pp. 702–5):

> The trouble with writing about something on the frontiers of knowledge is that the frontier is likely to move while you are writing. I had worked out much of what you have read when I made a light-hearted call to Dr Marquis, to ask whether there was anything new on the 'shift-to-risk phenomenon'. 'Yes', he said. 'It turns out not to be a shift to risk. Nordhoy has written some problems for which the decision after discussion is more cautious than the mean of the individual decisions. Isn't that interesting?' ...
> After some weeks of not-thinking, denial, somatic conversion, and derogation of the source I felt well enough to learn the details of Nordhoy's interesting results. ...
> Apparently group decisions on problems involving risk are sometimes riskier than the mean of prior individual decisions, sometimes more cautious, and sometimes not significantly different from the mean. ... We value both risk and caution, according to the circumstances.

It is heartening to see the psychologist reach firm ground at last, but he could save himself, and others, much time and effort if he were better informed about the location of the frontiers of knowledge.

This is only one, specially selected, case; and it does not demonstrate that the psychologist's conclusions are always, or even often, mistaken when they run counter to common sense. But my aim is to alert the reader to the possibility that such cases may be much more frequent than he might suppose. The most satisfactory way of showing that the danger is real would be for some other psychologist – one opposed to my views – to select cases which he considered to be genuinely new and valuable contributions. If these could be shown to be open to my criticisms, the case would be greatly strengthened. Fortunately, such an opportunity has recently presented itself; for one psychologist, Brand (1971), has listed what he considers to be significant findings, specifically to refute those critics like myself who have been protesting that much modern psychology is trivial or worse. If these examples can be shown to be unsatisfactory, it will be plain that the case is a strong one.

1 'High-status communicators are more persuasive'

This means that we are more likely to accept the statements and opinions of people in high places than those of Tom, Dick and Harry. In so far as there is some truth in this, it is in no way surprising. Such people have often attained their positions because they are exceptionally able in their fields. Naturally their views command respect. Leaders, one might say, have prestige. ('Influence, reputation, derived from past achievements, associations, etc.' *OED*.) But it is also obvious, I think, that this generalization has severe limits. If it were invariably true, it would be impossible to understand how the Left ever won an election. Clearly many factors besides high-status contribute to a man's persuasiveness, and sometimes – during the French Revolution for instance – high-status may have the opposite effect. When translated into plain English, this generalization is readily seen to be a half-truth, in which the true and the false are equally evident.

2 'Restrictions on communication result in lower satisfaction for the isolated'

One can agree that people do not like being sent to Coventry, or relish solitary confinement. But again there are obvious qualifications to be made. There are circumstances – a crowded beach or a packed train – where many people would prefer more privacy; and there are people – writers or monks – who actively seek solitude. Certainly people like company and conversation, and so restrictions on communication may result in lower satisfaction for the isolated. But they also like privacy and solitude, so restrictions may result in higher satisfaction for the overcrowded. It varies from person to person, and from occasion to occasion. This generalization again is a readily recognizable half-truth.

3 '*The major dimensions of personality (following Eysenck) are reasonably stable over time and may be used to predict a wide variety of anti-social and neurotic behaviours*'

This is in a somewhat different category since special knowledge of Eysenck's claims is necessary to assess it. However, in the first place, the claim is not in all respects as original as might be supposed. Eysenck himself has said that there is 'considerable agreement' between his system for describing the varieties of personality and the ancient doctrine of the four humours – sanguine, melancholic, choleric and phlegmatic (Eysenck, 1965, p. 54). It is commonly held, however, that the psychologist has brought a new accuracy of definition and measurement to distinctions which were in the past vague and qualitative, and that in consequence a valuable practical contribution can now be made. But such confident pronouncements need to be balanced against the more cautious estimates of other experts in the field. P. E. Vernon has expressed the view that it may be doubted whether clinicians or psychometricians have 'succeeded in providing acceptable and practicable methods of diagnosis which are consistently more accurate than the unsophisticated methods that we ordinarily use in understanding people in daily life' (Vernon, 1964, p. vii). Where the experts disagree, it is sensible to prefer the more cautious.

4 '*Exposure leads to attraction*'

Various interpretations of this law of nature may suggest themselves. It refers, I believe, to a view associated with Homans that people who are in frequent contact come to like each other. I do not know how the authors of such statements reconcile them with the numerous occasions when repeated contact leads to dislike, where familiarity breeds contempt.

Clearly, 'exposure' to people is a necessary condition for learning either to like or dislike them. If we like someone, we tend to prolong and renew the contact; if we dislike them, we tend to shorten and avoid it. Hence it would be more sensible to reverse the generalization, and say that liking leads to contact, though this is hardly informative.

These four generalizations were deliberately chosen to refute the critics of contemporary psychology, but since not one of them withstands examination, we can only conclude that the position of the critic must be strong. With respect, therefore, to the layman's first objection – that he could easily have worked it out for himself – it seems only too likely that he is often justified. Indeed, it seems that we may sometimes have to go further. We must be prepared, not only for the possibility that the psychologist's conclusions may not improve upon ordinary good sense, but also for the possibility that they may sometimes be distinctly inferior.

If the layman's understanding had been given its due, these pitfalls would have been foreseen. But the psychologist's rejection of it also has another unfortunate consequence. We may approach this second consequence by considering a comment which many psychologists might make about our discussion of the first consequence.

It might be pointed out, perfectly correctly, that the examples we have given of the first consequence come mainly from complex problems in human psychology – from child rearing or the determination of attitudes, from human character or social interaction. These are areas with which ordinary good sense is familiar, and here (our critic might agree) the psychologist's conclusions are sometimes open to the objection that we knew it all before. But large parts of psychology (the critic might continue) deal with very different matters – with animal behaviour or physiological mechanisms, with sense perception or reaction times. In these fields, it might be said, there are a large number of new and valuable scientific contributions to the explanation of behaviour, and it would be absurd to suggest that ordinary good sense might have anticipated these.

We shall later argue that this suggestion is by no means absurd, and that here too we often find our everyday modes of understanding hidden away beneath the technical terminology.

THE LAYMAN'S UNDERSTANDING

But certainly we can agree that the importance of everyday understanding is less obvious in these fields. Consequently, the first objection which the layman made – that he knew it all before – is seldom met. But the very fact that ordinary understanding is *not* in evidence, brings out another objection. What, the layman asks, have these studies to do with psychology? In his view, whatever else psychology may do, it should contribute to the understanding of human nature. By 'the understanding of human nature' he means the understanding which we all possess in daily life. Thus he expects that the understanding which the psychologist offers will bear some relation to the understanding which he himself already has. If the psychologist offers explanations which bear no relation to this, or if the psychologist suggests or implies that his everyday understanding is of no significance, the layman is inevitably puzzled or dissatisfied. But the fields of psychology to which we have just referred often seem to the layman to lack this connection; and sometimes they seem to be pursued to the detriment, and even to the exclusion, of what he thinks should be the primary aim. The layman – and in this case the layman is most often the student – concludes that psychology is failing to do the job it ought to do.

But psychologists are familiar with this objection too, just as they were with the first. An answer was given several years ago by Zangwill, and has been widely followed since. In an introductory book, he explained frankly that many problems of the 'greatest interest' to the student would find 'scant mention', and stated that he would give 'little attention' to personality, and 'none whatever' to social psychology. He continued as follows (Zangwill, 1950, p. viii):

> These omissions are certainly not due to any lack of interest on my part or on that of psychologists in general. They are due to my belief that scientific study to date has added little that is new to our understanding of these problems. As yet, the scientific study of personality is in its infancy, and social psychology remains a dream rather than an accepted discipline.

These blunt comments, it will be noted, are entirely in accordance with the conclusions which we have ourselves just reached about much work in these areas; and we shall shortly return to this point. Here it may be mentioned that Zangwill, who adopts the biological standpoint, then recommends his readers to study experimental and physiological psychology, suggesting that these will form the 'hard core of the psychology of tomorrow' (ibid.).

It is clearly views such as this which tend to produce the kind of psychology which evokes the layman's second objection. But ought the layman to be satisfied with this answer? At first sight, it might seem that the answer is eminently reasonable; that if scientific study to date has added little that is new, there can be little of significance to discuss, and we must contain our impatience. But this argument assumes that only what is scientific can be worth the attention of the psychologist, and that scientific study will one day contribute something of importance. It implies that the principle invoked – that only what is scientific is admissible – is only a device for ensuring that conclusions when they come will be reliable. These assumptions may be questioned. It is arguable that the principle in fact leads to the active exclusion of these topics, however interested the psychologist may personally feel, and that it actually makes reliable or significant work in these fields extremely difficult, if not impossible.

The closer we approach to human psychology, and especially to such central topics as personality and social psychology, the more obvious it becomes that we already possess an extensive everyday knowledge of the subject. It is here that our self-understanding operates at its most conspicuous and successful. But this, as we have seen, comes into conflict with the scientific approach as it is conventionally cultivated. Accordingly the first step in the scientific education of the student is often to undermine his conviction of the importance and reliability of the understanding which he already has, and to suggest that his layman's interest in human nature is inappropriate in a scientific discipline. As Kohler remarked, the layman's conviction 'plays hardly any part in the scientific psychology of our time' (1947, p. 322). Or as Skinner said: 'It is science or nothing' (1972, p. 160). Consequently we can well understand how it is that a recent review of two leading textbooks of psychology written from the biological standpoint – those by Galanter (1966) and Hebb (1966) – should feel it necessary to comment that 'a determined wish to kill a perfectly legitimate interest in human nature which the student may bring to the study of psychology is evidently the first wish of both authors' (Lawlor, 1967). The critic of much contemporary psychology may justly object that the very interest which brought the student to psychology in the first place, and the very capacity which might stand him in good stead in its study, must both be frustrated before what is called his scientific education can begin.

We began by suggesting that the layman's understanding of human nature is both extensive and reliable, and that it would be disastrous for the psychologist to neglect this most remarkable and distinctive characteristic of human beings. We then found that the scientific psychologist is prone not merely to neglect it, but to oppose it. We have also found that the layman often reacts to psychology with two critical comments: sometimes he objects that he knew it all before; at other times he objects that it does not seem to be concerned with human nature.

These two criticisms, though contrasted, are not unrelated; and it is not difficult to see how they arise. Psychologists are predominantly trained to approach their subject from the standpoint of biological science. This teaches them to neglect the layman's understanding, and often encourages them to concentrate their efforts in areas which are remote from human nature. This naturally gives rise to the objection that much psychology fails to deal with its proper subject. But if now some of these psychologists attempt to use such a training to throw light on human nature, we can hardly be surprised if they must first discover what the layman knew before, and we must even be prepared for the possibility that they will not get as far. We can also see that the more cautious exponents of scientific psychology may well feel hesitant about the attempts of their more confident colleagues to tackle problems in human personality and social interaction; while the more confident may feel some impatience with the more cautious for their failure to face the most challenging problems.

Clearly a more thorough study of the aims and methods of psychology is required, especially in relation to the layman's claim. But from this preliminary examination, scientific psychology does not yet inspire our confidence. It rejects man's most distinctive feature, but seems to have little to put in its place. At this point the reader, who may have heard confident claims for modern psychology, will perhaps ask himself whether so critical a judgment can be well founded. This is a question to be considered in the light of our subsequent argument; meanwhile, we may recall that Gibson, a leading American psychologist, has remarked (1967, p. 142) that psychologists

seem to feel, many of them, that all we need to do is consolidate our scientific gains. Their self-confidence astonishes me. For these gains seem to me puny, and scientific psychology seems to me ill-founded. At any time the whole psychological applecart might be upset. Let them beware.

2
THE REJECTION OF MIND

How did psychology fall into this disastrous situation, in which
it neglects the cardinal feature of human nature? The answer
to this question must be sought in its history. If we go back to
the end of the nineteenth century, we find that the psychology
of those days was in fact concerned to study man's understanding of himself and the world. But this study met various
difficulties and objections, until eventually, in the early years of
this century, it was largely abandoned in favour of alternative
views, of which behaviourism was the chief. It was in this way
that the layman's conviction came to play so small a part in
modern psychology. This book will suggest that the concepts
and methods in which modern psychology has placed its faith
have now unquestionably broken down. In this situation, we
have much to learn from the older tradition, which had already
attempted the task which we now face.

Everyday talk about behaviour refers to what is usually
called 'mental life'. 'Why did you invite him to lunch?'
'Because I did not want to hurt his feelings'. . . . 'Why did you
go back?' 'Because I remembered I had a letter to post'. . . .

'What are you going to do this afternoon?' 'I have decided I must attend that meeting.' Such remarks refer to thoughts, feelings, wishes, recollections, intentions and innumerable other shades of mental activity. In daily life, this activity usually presents few problems: each phase grows smoothly and comprehensibly from that which went before. It is not a meaningless succession of unrelated events, of which we are the helpless spectators. It is our own personal and familiar experience, in which we are the active and insightful agents.

But however comprehensible it seems as we live through it, mental life becomes puzzling when we reflect upon it. When we take it for granted, nothing could be more straightforward. When we examine it, nothing could be more elusive. The problems are often philosophical rather than psychological, though the borderline between the two is rough and uncertain, and each has far-reaching implications for the other. This is particularly obvious with respect to the most insoluble problems of all, which arise from the contrast between mental life and other things. A philosopher expresses the contrast as follows (Flew, 1965, p. 112):

> On the one side there are the questions, answers, concepts and explanations which refer to mechanisms and other things incapable of purpose, intention, rationality. . . . The home of this first category . . . is the sphere of technology and of the physical and biological sciences, although no one disputes that there is at least some scope for them in considering some aspects of the human organism. . . . On the other side we have those questions, answers, concepts and explanations which refer to reasons, purposes, wishes, intentions, and so on. These belong to the human studies, such as history, and to everyday discourse about conduct.

From this contrast comes the perennial problem of the nature of mind and its relation to the material world. In its narrower aspect, this concerns the relation of mind and body; in its broader aspect, it concerns the relation of mind to the world in general, especially with respect to the nature and validity of human knowledge. Psychology is inevitably affected by the solutions which philosophers propose to these questions, for these entail conclusions about the kinds of explanations which are appropriate. At the same time, philosophy must take account of the description of mental life which psychology provides. Consequently, philosophy and psychology have often in the past been thoroughly mixed up together, and attempts to pursue them in isolation from each other have rarely continued successfully for very long.

This prepares us for the form in which psychology was traditionally conceived. During the eighteenth and nineteenth centuries, it was generally regarded as the study of mental life, and was pursued in close association with philosophy. As such, it conformed to the layman's expectations, at least in so far as its subject matter was concerned. What the psychologist made of that subject matter might often have seemed obscure or artificial to the layman; but it tried to do justice to an aspect of his experience which he could recognize as worth attention. At the same time, its close connection with philosophy was a permanent reminder that this inquiry was never far from questions of far-reaching significance which could not be expected to yield to quick or easy answers. It is impossible to characterize this traditional psychology in a brief space, but one may perhaps point to certain leading features which are often, in my opinion, misunderstood or neglected in such a way as to discredit a tradition which still has much to teach us.

The first concerns the gradual evolution of psychological thought during this period. Its history is largely that of a continual interplay between two contrasting points of view, represented by the theory of faculties and the theory of association. The former treated mental life as the expression of certain natural powers and capacities; the latter attempted to analyse mental life into its supposed components and to trace these to previous experience. Originally stated in relatively simple terms, these points of view were gradually elaborated and refined in the light of mutual criticism. In such an extensive tradition, it is not difficult to find examples of work which is in many ways defective. But it can only be adequately judged by examining the best work which it produced, and this is to be found in its culmination at the end of the nineteenth century, and especially in the writings of such men as James, Ward and Stout. This marks a great advance over earlier ways of thinking, and in comparison with it much contemporary writing seems shallow.

The second feature concerns the methods used. It is frequently suggested that each psychologist examined his own mental processes in isolation, took his observations as indubitable, and then indulged a taste for dogmatic speculation. Certainly, their primary source was introspection – the perception of what takes place within our own mind. But the difficulties and dangers of this method were often stressed. James remarked that it was like turning the gas up quickly to see what the darkness looked like. But this did not prevent him from saying that 'Introspective Observation is what we have to rely on first and foremost and always' (1890, p. 185). Rather, the difficulties led to a realization that it was essential for each psychologist to pay careful attention to the findings of others, and to regard his study as one in which results were gradually accumulated from one generation to the next. Stout expressed this need for confirmation in the following words, which are particularly notable in view of subsequent arguments (1896, 1, p. 14):

> In physical science an observation made by one person and unconfirmed by others is regarded as valueless. I have no hesitation in saying that in psychology we should be no less rigid. No general principle can be legitimately accepted on the evidence of introspection or retrospection alone, unless it has been corroborated by a consensus of experts.

Another source of data lay in the observation of behaviour, or the outward signs of mental life. Stout described this as 'immensely important' (ibid., p. 13), but also regarded it as a secondary and derivative method, since the mental life of others can only be inferred, not directly observed. By the end of the nineteenth century the student of the introspective tradition would have found many points which were uncertain or obscure, but he would also have found that it carried him much farther and faster than he could have travelled on his own.

The third feature of the traditional psychology concerns its rapid growth towards the end of the nineteenth century. Many new areas of study were added to its traditional field, and it became clear that this foreshadowed far-reaching changes. The method of introspection is chiefly appropriate in studying the mental life of the adult human being, and the civilized and stable man at that. But clearly this is a special form of mental

C

life, and needs to be considered in relation to many other expressions of mind. Children, primitive peoples, the mentally disordered or defective, and animal life in general, may all claim a place, perhaps a most important place, in the study of mind. But in all these cases introspection is either doubtful or impossible, and we must recognize that the observation of behaviour is likely to play a more dominant role. In addition to these developments, there was also to be considered the general progress of the natural sciences, and the increasing relevance of physiological inquiry in particular. The idea of evolution began to exert a profound influence on psychological thought, while the possibility of experiment became increasingly attractive. As the end of the century approached, it became clear that the traditional introspective psychology must be considered in a far wider framework than hitherto.

It seemed to Stout that the importance of the introspective psychology was enhanced not diminished now that it was no longer the whole of psychology, but only a fragment of it. He recognized that the new points of view each had its own distinct and independent ways of collecting and estimating evidence, but this opened the possibility that the traditional psychology could in future be useful, not only within its accepted field, but also as a help to these newer movements. This help, he suggested, was 'comparable to the guidance which an inland explorer of a large island may receive from a chart of the coast' (Stout, 1896, 1, p. ix). It was certainly very much in this spirit that many of the pioneers of the new movements in psychology regarded the introspective tradition. When Wundt founded the first psychological laboratory at Leipzig in 1879 he regarded it primarily as a place in which introspection could be conducted more carefully and systematically; and Lloyd Morgan considered that the study of animal behaviour must proceed by analogy and inference from our introspective knowledge of the developed forms of mental life in man. The stage was being set for a general advance of psychology, in which a diversity of approaches could be harmoniously related round its traditional centre.

But just as these favourable prospects seemed to be opening ahead, psychology encountered a problem which led first to bitter controversy and eventually to a radical break with tradition. The difficulty arose through the increasing influence of the scientific outlook, and from the circumstance that this outlook introduced convictions which were at variance with those which had so far been accepted. Those who came to psychology with a training in the natural sciences, or with a sympathy for the scientific modes of explanation, naturally preferred the mechanical categories which had proved so successful in physics and biology. It seemed to them to be axiomatic that psychology should attempt to model itself upon those sciences. But these explanations, as we have just noted, stand in marked contrast to explanations in terms of reasons, purposes, wishes and intentions. Thus the whole conception of mental life began to seem to them to be something which stood in the way of a properly scientific inquiry. This general preference was reinforced by a frequent experience of scientific men. In the past, explanations of the mentalistic character had not been confined to the human studies. Natural phenomena had often been explained in 'animistic' terms, in which 'spirits' were responsible for everything from eclipses to earthquakes. The scientist had sometimes to face great hostility before these explanations would be surrendered and his own explanations accepted. The controversy surrounding the substitution of Natural Selection for Divine Creation provided a contemporary instance, or at least was widely seen as such. Thus to psychologists with a scientific bent it came to seem, not merely that mechanical explanations were preferable, but that the progress of science must be expected to entail the gradual elimination of all reference to mental life. The introduction of wishes, purposes, intentions and so on came increasingly to seem to be a reprehensible, indeed a superstitious, departure from the proper scientific path. In the course of his *Principles of Psychology*, James recorded: 'I have heard a most intelligent biologist say: "It is high time for scientific men to protest against the recognition of any such thing as consciousness in a scientific investigation"' (1890, p. 134). When this conviction was combined with the further belief that in psychology, as elsewhere, scientific investigation was alone admissible, the stage was set for a radical challenge to the view that psychology was to be regarded as the study of mental life.

In this context, there were two further considerations to which the scientist could appeal. First, he could draw a most unfavourable comparison between the achievements of psychology, and those of the natural sciences. Psychology lacked precise and quantitative methods; it lacked general theories of wide and proven explanatory power; it could not compete with respect to predictive capacity or practical application. On the contrary, it had always been divided between rival standpoints; it was too often pre-occupied with philosophical puzzles which issued in no clear solutions; and there were certain important respects in which it could not even agree on its facts, such as the place of imagery in thought. It might have been said in defence that the scientist was applying standards which were inappropriate in psychology; but one can readily appreciate that the scientist, aware of the great achievements of the natural sciences, would have little patience with such a reply.

But second the scientist could point particularly to the progress of physiology during the nineteenth century. The principle of reflex action provided a means of explaining certain simple forms of behaviour without appealing to the memory or intelligence of the agent; and it began to seem plausible that eventually, as knowledge of nervous function grew, it would be possible to explain even the most complex behaviour in a similar way. But the brain and nervous system must be regarded as physicochemical, no different in fundamentals from any other material structure, and subject to the same ultimate laws as every other part of nature. Thus while the traditional psychology might be depicted as a failure, the growth of physiology might be represented as offering a prospect of incorporating psychology within the system of science.

In this situation it began to seem that the only acceptable explanation of human behaviour itself must be explanation in terms of the action of the brain. The 'layman's conviction' – and all understanding which belongs to the human studies and to everyday discourse about conduct – came to seem an unscientific irrelevance. So we find that a 'new psychology' was increasingly opposed to the old. It did not at first go so far as James's biologist, and demand that there should be no reference to consciousness. A less drastic doctrine, termed epiphenomenalism, was at first preferred. This allowed that consciousness or mental life existed, and could be included in psychological inquiry. But it held that consciousness was a mere by-product of brain activity. It was produced by brain action, but was not itself capable of any reciprocal reaction. The belief that mental events could influence the action of the brain was in any case incomprehensible, for no one could explain how the immaterial could affect the material. Mental life was no more responsible for the determination of behaviour, than the smoke from an engine determined its speed or direction. The task of psychology was simply to discover what neural events corresponded to what mental events, and nothing more.

These views were strongly attacked. James argued that if mental life had no causal efficacy, it could contribute nothing to the struggle for survival, and hence no reason could be given why it should have evolved. In a famous passage, he pointed out some further consequences of the 'automaton-theory'. On this view, it would be possible in principle to predict everything which Shakespeare ever wrote, if we had sufficient knowledge of his brain, without in the least comprehending what passed through his mind when he wrote it; and 'in like manner we might exhaustively write the biography of those two hundred pounds, more or less, of warmish albuminoid matter called Martin Luther, without ever implying that it felt' (James, 1890, pp. 132-3). All this was to be accepted because nobody could explain how mental life could affect bodily behaviour. And yet, as James pointed out, if this causal relation was obscure, it was no more obscure than its counterpart – how the action of the brain produced mental life. But this was accepted by the epiphenomenalist without question. In the present state of psychology, concluded James, the automaton-theory was an 'unwarrantable impertinence' (ibid., p. 138).

The consequences for psychology of adopting this standpoint were examined also by G. F. Stout. In his *Analytic Psychology*, he referred to the belief of certain physiologists that 'the only way of explaining the phenomena of consciousness is by connecting them with the physical phenomena of the brain and nervous system', and to their belief that, if this were accomplished, psychology would be 'absorbed in physiology' (1, p. 3). Stout argued that the consequences would be more disastrous. He wrote as follows (1896, 1, pp. 3-4):

The distinctive aim of the psychologist is to investigate mental events themselves, not their mechanical accompaniments or antecedents. If the course of mental events is not regulated by discoverable uniformities capable of being interconnected so as to form a coherent system, the psychologist has nothing to do. It is incorrect to say that on this assumption his science becomes absorbed in physiology. It does not become absorbed; it simply ceases to exist in any form whatever.

It should be stressed that this argument does not refute epiphenomenalism. It only asserts that a genuine psychology must bring to light meaningful relations among mental events themselves. Epiphenomenalism rules out this possibility, because if the only way of explaining consciousness is by connecting it with the brain, each successive mental state will be explained in turn as arising from the corresponding brain state. On this view, it is permissible to look for connections between successive brain states, but not between successive mental states: there is a task here for the physiologist, but not for the psychologist. Thus the truth of epiphenomenalism is left open, for the psychologist cannot legitimately argue that a view is false because it leaves him without employment. But it does show that a man cannot legitimately accept epiphenomenalism, and still call himself a psychologist; and it indicates what psychology must entail, if it is to be possible.

The ideal of the natural scientist was that psychology should one day be incorporated in the system of knowledge which the physical sciences were gradually building, which had for its object the material world considered as a single continuous mechanical system. But in this system there could be, in Stout's view, no place for psychology. The aim of psychology was essentially distinct from that of the physical sciences. They were concerned to acquire knowledge of the material world, but psychology was concerned to study how such knowledge comes into being. Thus 'physical science might conceivably be carried to a high degree of completeness apart from any implied advance in psychology, because we might have perfect knowledge of the material world and yet remain ignorant of the process through which such knowledge had arisen' (Stout, 1896, 1, p. 7). As to the relations of the knower and the known, James remarked that these 'are infinitely complicated, and that a genial, whole-hearted, popular-science way of formulating them will not suffice' (James, 1892, p. 333).

Epiphenomenalism may perhaps be seen as a half-way house towards a more thorough rejection of mental life. For although it treated consciousness as a by-product, it still recognized its existence. It did not meet fully the requirement of James's biologist, that scientific men should refuse to recognize any such thing as consciousness in a scientific investigation. It was soon to be succeeded by another 'new psychology', with a fresh recipe, and this time the traditional views were to be swept aside.

The doctrine which was to be widely hailed as finally incorporating psychology within the system of natural science, came in 1912 when J. B. Watson first enunciated the principles of behaviourism. His programme was a double one: first, to reject the traditional conception of psychology as the study of mental life; and second, to substitute the conception of psychology as the science of behaviour. Watson's formulations brought to a head the tension which had been growing between the time-honoured procedures of the classical psychologists and the newer methods of natural science. The adherents of the scientific standpoint seem to have felt a need to stake their claim forcibly by demanding a new departure, and certainly Watson met with an immediate and enthusiastic response. Behaviourism was by no means the only movement of the period, but it rapidly became established as the dominant tendency of modern psychology.

The rejection of mental life was expressed in the most forthright terms. 'The time seems to have come,' wrote Watson, 'when psychology must discard all reference to consciousness, when it need no longer delude itself into thinking that it is making mental states the object of observation' (Watson, 1914, p. 7). He argued that the subject matter of a science must be publicly or objectively verifiable. But mental states were private to each individual, so that the deliverances of introspection could never be verified. It is sometimes suggested that Watson did not wish to deny the existence of mental life, but only to urge that it had no place in a scientific psychology. But all that matters is that he was adamant that it should be ejected from psychology. 'If behaviourism is ever to stand for anything,' he asserted, 'it must make a clean break with the whole concept of consciousness' (Watson, 1924a, p. viii).

Thus Watson may be seen as completing the trend which epiphenomenalism had begun. He has gone beyond the view that psychology should seek the physiological determinants of mental states, for mental states are nowhere permitted to enter into the equation, even in the humble role of superfluous by-product. Watson saw himself as making a clean and final break with the mystifications of the old tradition. It is important to notice that it was not merely the philosophical psychology which incurred his hostility. He was equally opposed to the views of Wundt, who had so recently introduced experiment, for Wundt still accepted the use of introspection. Indeed, there was an important respect in which Watson had more in common with Stout than he had with Wundt. For Wundt had supposed that experimental introspection could pave the way for the incorporation of psychology in the natural sciences. Watson, on the other hand, was denying the possibility of a science of mental life. But this, of course, was Stout's position. The difference between Watson and Stout was that Stout wished to persevere with the study of mental life as an inquiry distinct from natural science; whereas Watson was convinced that only a natural science could prove satisfactory, and therefore rejected the concept of mind. But both agreed that mental life escaped the categories and methods of physical science.

Watson considered that when behaviour was substituted for mind, the old difficulties would disappear. Behaviour was objectively observable, and psychology could restrict itself to the search for the objective conditions of behaviour. The problem of mind and body no longer obtruded into the picture. There was still a question, however, about the relation between psychology and physiology. It might have been supposed that the immediate determinants of behaviour were to be found in brain action, and so it might have seemed that it would now be the task of the physiologist to explain behaviour, and that behaviourism, like epiphenomenalism, would leave the psychologist no function. Watson did not deny that brain events were the immediate cause, but a sphere was found for psychology through the famous stimulus-response formula. Every response is elicited by a stimulus. The task of psychology is to establish the relations between them: given the stimulus, to predict the response; or, given the response, to state what the stimulus must have been. The stimulus is connected with the response through the nervous system, and this is the province of physiology. But psychology could establish its stimulus-response generalizations independently of a knowledge of the nervous connections, leaving it to physiology to discover these in due course. This might be expressed by saying that psychology is concerned with the activities of the organism as a whole, whereas physiology is mainly interested in the functions of the parts of the body taken separately.

Behaviourism entailed a revolution in the standpoint from which psychology was to be studied. The centre of gravity of the subject was to be shifted bodily into the biological sciences. The starting-point was no longer to be the introspective study of human mental life, but the experimental and objective examination of the simplest forms of behaviour. As these were gradually mastered, there would be a firm foundation from which to approach the more complex behaviour of man. Watson himself could only offer the blueprint of the new science, but now that the old misconceptions had been removed, it seemed to many that its gradual emergence could be anticipated with confidence. But this new standpoint implied that the layman's understanding could be safely ignored, and the consequences of neglecting it remained to be seen.

The introspective tradition, of course, retained some adherents, who protested strongly against these new tendencies. Ward regarded the attempt to treat psychology from the standpoint of physical science as disastrous: 'As a *method* in the hands of psychologists it has done some good; as a pretended *science* in the hands of tyros whose psychological training has not even begun, it has done infinite harm' (Ward, 1918, p. vii; see also 1893). But despite the critics, behaviourism exerted an extremely wide and powerful influence. There were indeed other movements, such as psychoanalysis and *Gestalt* theory, which were deeply opposed to behaviourism. But it was the behaviourists who set the distinctive tone of modern psychology, especially in academic circles. Their influence was marked even among those who would not have cared to call themselves behaviourists, showing itself in a tendency to refer to introspection with some hesitation, as a method supplementary to objective observation of behaviour, no longer as something to be relied on 'first and

29

foremost and always' as it had been for James. So we may next ask how this dominant movement looks today, from the standpoint of a contemporary behaviourist.

Broadbent's *Behaviour*, written in 1961, may be taken as representative of the position which the modern behaviourist adopts. Broadbent states that there are certain important respects in which the original views of Watson have undergone modification, especially with respect to the theory of learning, and to the significance which is now attached to heredity. But Watson is treated as the key figure in the history of psychology, from whom the modern science of behaviour stems. Watson's central ideas – the rejection of mental life, and the substitution of the stimulus-response formula – are retained, as of course they must be if the title 'behaviourist' is to be justified.

We have already seen that, in Broadbent's opinion, the experience of the layman and humanist education are of little significance for scientific psychology. This is presented at the outset in the following way. Broadbent states that our usual frame of reference 'distinguishes sharply between an impersonal world and an internal, acutely personal, one'; and he adds that 'the concepts employed within the latter – wishes, anxieties, memories – are altogether different in kind from those used to describe the physical world' (Broadbent, 1961, p. 10). It might have been expected that, as a psychologist, Broadbent would then indicate that psychology is concerned with this inner personal world, and that, having stressed the difference between this and the impersonal material world, he would advise us to approach these two worlds differently, or at least to be cautious if we attempted to treat them similarly. But, as a behaviourist, Broadbent wishes to justify 'turning away from conscious experience towards behaviour' (ibid., p. 35). He considers that 'the most hopeful road is to apply to behaviour itself the method of attack which has proved so useful in dealing with the material world' (ibid., p. 9); and he recommends us to 'develop the analysis of behaviour in terms which refer to the public world rather than to the inner one' (ibid., p. 11).

Broadbent refers to those psychologists who 'would prefer to use, as explanations, ideas drawn from the ordinary vocabulary men use to describe their experience; to speak of a certain action as explained by the hope, or repulsion, or imaginative insight of the man who performs it' (ibid., p. 37). But concerning this trust in the language of everyday experience, he writes (ibid., p. 37):

> But despite its attractiveness, and the worthy motives of those who use it, the modern behaviourist believes that its use in serious study of human beings is based on a logical fallacy. At least this is true if no special steps are taken to redefine and purge the words of common speech so that they take on an uncommon meaning.

Using common words with an uncommon meaning is as good a recipe for confusion as could well be invented, but Broadbent is in fact concerned with the importance of clear definition. The fallacy to which he refers is, apparently, that one cannot convey directly what is in one's mind; rather, one must define what is meant in terms of observed events. By 'observed events' he means events in the public, material, world – 'situations to which a man must respond, and actions or words which he produces' (ibid., p. 41). This prepares the way for a statement of the stimulus-response formula which is the same as that which the behaviourists have always proposed, for Broadbent concludes his argument by writing: 'So we reach the view of a science which relates events at the bodily senses ("stimuli") to events at those parts of the body which act on the outer world ("responses")' (ibid., p. 41).

Finally, Broadbent shows no lack of confidence in the claims which he makes for the behaviourist approach. The method of objective experiment is a 'generally accepted doctrine' (ibid., p. 35); and 'there is no other way (besides the behaviourist one) of attaining certain knowledge of other men' (p. 47). This approach 'is bound to cause an upheaval in our ideas about human personality' (p. 10); and 'the advance of this branch of science threatens to make an impact upon our philosophies which will be at least as great as the impact of Darwinism' (p. 11).

Despite its widespread influence, behaviourism has never gained that universal acceptance which is the hallmark of a successful scientific revolution. In origin, it was a recipe for a suitable method of formulating and testing psychological theories, rather than a well articulated series of hypotheses.

And its subsequent history has been marked by a succession of controversial attempts to elaborate a theory, not by the appearance of a definitive version. Thus it is the method of objective experiment which Broadbent claims as a 'generally accepted doctrine', and not any clearly defined system of explanatory principles which have been verified by this method.

We shall shortly attempt a critical examination of the method of objective experiment; but in order to prepare the reader we may notice here a feature of behaviourist thinking which is not always given the attention it deserves. Watson, and many of his followers, write as if there would be no great difficulty in ridding ourselves of mental concepts. Once the intellectual decision has been taken, it should be a simple matter, they suppose, to confine ourselves to objective observation. But this assumption is highly misleading. The use of mental concepts is not a philosophical importation which we can abandon at will. It is deeply ingrained in our habits of thought, and pervades every observation and every interpretation which we make of human behaviour. Our very perception of behaviour is riddled through and through with attributions of mental life. When we describe a man as smiling, hesitating, waiting, looking, threatening, pausing, approaching, avoiding, nodding or cringing, we are describing his behaviour as the expression of the mental life of an experiencing agent. To describe it objectively – that is, as sheer bodily change, as 'colourless movement' – demands an effort of abstraction of which most people, including most behaviourists, are wholly incapable. Hence we must not for one moment imagine that the behaviourists are going to be able to live up to their declared intentions. On the contrary, the 'objective' observation which they will offer will prove to be saturated with the mental life they profess to have discarded. Behaviourism ignores the layman's conviction, but the penalty for this temerity is to find yourself the unwitting exponent of its claims.

This point may be illustrated by considering the way in which Broadbent himself estimates the behaviourist achievement when he reaches the end of his account. His initial revolutionary claims seem now to have given way to a rather different tune. He writes as follows (op. cit., p. 178):

A large number of facts have emerged, some surprising, and some in accordance with the traditional wisdom of experienced men. Indeed, it can hardly have escaped the reader that these experimental results should produce no radical change in the normal practice of sensitive people when dealing with their fellows. . . . The merit of objective study is that it provides a means of testing intuitive know-ledge and sorting out the true from the false; not that it should necessarily provide some quite different and previously unheard of method of dealing with people.

But this is not the upheaval which we were led to expect; and if we examine the results in more detail, we shall find, I believe, that they are even less notable than the above passage suggests. A field to which behaviourists have devoted enormous energy and resources is learning, specifically animal learning. Broadbent summarizes much of the work in this area with the following 'general conclusion' (ibid., p. 75):

The rough idea, that actions followed by reward are repeated, is one which is likely to occur to most intelligent people who think about possible explanations of behaviour. As we have seen, it is approximately true but must be stated very carefully. Some of the obvious possible theories, such as the idea that large and obvious rewards will be better than very indirect and concealed ones, have already been disproved by experiment. There remain a number of others which have not, and there are no good grounds for supporting one of them rather than another.

There are a number of points to be made about this passage, which is representative of much contemporary psychology. When Broadbent describes this 'rough idea' as 'one which is likely to occur to most intelligent people', he understates the case. Has there ever existed a people so primitive that they have not grasped this feature of human nature? Broadbent is suggesting that the psychologist who notes this principle is operating much closer to what Brown called 'the frontiers of knowledge' than is really the case. Again, the use of the term 'reward' is a clear example of a common word which implies a sentient subject, and which is not in fact being given an un-common meaning (since it would occur to most intelligent

33

people). Of course such principles have to be stated very carefully, as the traditional introspective psychology was at pains to point out. But I do not think that we can really be expected to believe that large and obvious rewards are not, in general, better than very indirect and concealed ones. Few employers would last very long, if for large and obvious pay packets, they substituted small post-dated cheques which the worker had to hunt for round the factory. I can believe that there may be circumstances when this does not hold, but this is a case where, if experiment is supposed to have disproved it, we have to be sensible enough to prefer common sense.

This provides a further instance, to be added to those mentioned in the first chapter, where the psychologist's findings seem either to be a mere repetition of what ordinary good sense already knew, or, regrettably, a distinctly inferior brand of information. There is also a further point. Broadbent is mainly concerned with animal behaviour. Thus the tendency to tell us what we knew before is not confined to psychologists who study the more complex problems of human psychology; it is also to be found in the biological foundations, as we suggested it might. Psychology, it seems, is a science which specializes not in discovery but in re-discovery.

Our next task is to examine the method of objective experiment. In doing so, it should be emphasized that the influence of behaviourism has spread far beyond those who would call themselves strict behaviourists. Just as the 'behaviourist's prejudice' has led to a general tendency to undervalue the subject's report, so there is a widespread belief that objective experiment is desirable, whether or not it is conducted from an explicitly behaviourist standpoint. As Broadbent says, it is a 'generally accepted doctrine'. In the past, the use of experiment in psychology has too often been presented with uncritical enthusiasm, and introductory texts in general still expound the method without reference to the special difficulties which are encountered. Thus we find it suggested that, however limited the theoretical contributions of experimental psychology may be, there are no intrinsic defects in the method itself. But there are many signs of a more critical approach. There is a growing literature on personal and social factors in psychological experiments, and the problems which they bring. (See Jung, 1971.) Experimentalists are themselves expressing reservations.

Thus Zangwill writes that 'experimental psychology has not wholly justified the earlier confidence placed in it as a department of science. . . . The whole conception of experiment in psychology awaits clarification' (Zangwill, 1964a, pp. 134–5).

Our own conclusions will perhaps be regarded as unduly negative. But he who attempts to clarify the method cannot stipulate in advance that the outcome must be satisfying. To criticize the method is to imply that it is worth criticizing, and that it should not be thrown aside thoughtlessly because it has not lived up to our expectations. It is to express the hope that we may in this way discover what we lack, and thereby find an escape from our difficulties.

3

THE BREAKDOWN OF OBJECTIVE
EXPERIMENT: OUTER CONDITIONS

There is agreement, in general terms, about what would constitute a satisfactory objective experiment. To experiment is to establish systematic control over the conditions operating in a given situation, in order to discover their relative contribution to some effect. In objective psychology, the effect is the subject's response or behaviour (termed the dependent variable), and the aim is to determine the conditions which control it (termed the independent variables). It is usual to distinguish two main classes of independent variables: those which are external to the organism, and those which are internal. Thus if the method is to be applied successfully, it is necessary to identify and control, with reasonable precision, the relevant external and internal conditions. It is also necessary to define the response.

But when we ask how the general principle is to be applied, we find that there is no single agreed and effective procedure. Instead, objective psychologists recommend a variety of practices, all of which are in various ways inadequate. The need for a clarification of the method becomes obvious. It will be argued that a main reason for this unsatisfactory state of affairs is that it proves in practice extremely difficult to give an objective definition of variables, whether dependent or independent. Part of the explanation of this difficulty is to be found in the distinction of outer and inner conditions. It has been widely recognized that inner conditions are relatively inaccessible, and present acute problems with respect to identification and control. We shall consider outer conditions first, reserving the question of inner conditions for the next chapter. The reader should be warned, however, that the distinction between outer and inner is a slippery one. It often happens that what purports to be an objective description of the external situation, in fact contains a great deal of human interpretation, and therefore is contributed by inner not outer conditions. This brings us to the general difficulty, already mentioned, which applies throughout: we are so used, in our daily life, to interpreting situations and behaviour in mentalistic terms, that this mode of thinking repeatedly insinuates itself into the discussion. Hence the accounts which the experimenter gives of his procedures and results, and the explanations which he attempts, owe far more than he realizes to the mentalistic understanding of everyday life. Instead of objective description, there is an unintended intrusion of mental concepts. Subjective interpretation, one might say, is masquerading as objective finding.

This tendency is greatly strengthened when human beings are used as subjects, for people naturally interpret the experimental situation in ways analogous to their interpretation of everyday situations, and behave in accordance with that understanding. If the subject speaks, the experimenter is exposed to this contamination; and special techniques are often used to protect him from it. Of these, the most important is the general tendency to disparage the subject's report; but they are rarely wholly effective, and our everyday habits of thought repeatedly infect the purity of objective experiment. It might be suggested that the remedy lies in the still more rigorous exclusion of mental life. But this is the cause of the trouble in the first place. A better solution is to recognize that psychology must concern itself with mental life, and examine these concepts openly.

We have mentioned that outer conditions are relatively easier to control than inner conditions, and we shall first consider the general significance of this. The point itself will be readily appreciated. We can decide how the laboratory shall be furnished, what apparatus shall be used, what instructions the subject shall be given, and so on. Certainly there are difficulties. Some of these are obvious, such as the problems involved in reproducing the more complex 'real-life' situations. Others are easy to overlook, such as the various subtle ways in which the experimenter may unintentionally indicate the kind of result he expects (the 'experimenter effects'; see Rosenthal, 1967). But real and important as these difficulties are, they are less acute than the problems posed by inner factors. Looked at in common-sensical terms, it is clear that the subject's behaviour will be influenced by his temperament and intelligence, by the general course of his past experience, and by particular motives or preconceptions which may be thrown up by the experimental situation. The inner conditions are represented by what the layman would call an enormous range of thoughts and feelings, which will plainly be very difficult to pin down. If, alternatively, the reader prefers to conceive these in physiological terms, it remains equally true that present techniques for controlling these are primitive, especially where human beings are concerned. Whatever may one day be the case, there can be no question that at present inner conditions present the experimenter with a daunting challenge.

At this point, there is a temptation for the experimentalist. If outer conditions are easier to control than inner, it would be highly advantageous if outer conditions were also more important in the determination of behaviour. For then – with outer conditions controlled, and inner conditions dismissed – the problem of conducting effective experiments in psychology might be regarded as substantially solved. In reality, it might be that a large and important class of variables – perhaps the most important – were being neglected, and that the experimenter was deluding himself that he had solved the problem when he had only scratched the surface.

This danger was discussed forty years ago by Sir Frederic Bartlett, perhaps the most eminent figure in the history of British experimental psychology, when he prefaced a book on *Remembering* with some reflections on experiment as it was then practised. He suggested that the pioneers of experimental psychology had been prone to this bias. They had attempted to 'control variations of response and experience by known variations of stimuli, and to explain the former in terms of the latter'. But this raised 'profound psychological difficulties. . . . The psychologist, of all people, should not stand in awe of the stimulus. . . . To make the explanation depend mainly upon variations of stimuli . . . is to ignore dangerously those equally important conditions of response which belong to the subjective attitude and to pre-determined reaction tendencies' (Bartlett, 1932, pp. 2–4). Bartlett attributed this tendency to the circumstance that so many of the pioneers had been trained initially in physics or physiology, and he regretted that their methods had, in his words (ibid., pp. 6–10):

> overspread the whole of psychological science. Yet all the while new problems, most of them concerned with conditions of response which have to be considered as resident within the organism – or the subject – itself have been forcing themselves to the front. . . . The external environment may remain constant, and yet the internal conditions of the reacting agent – the attitudes, moods, all that mass of determining factors which go under the names of temperament and character – may vary significantly. These, however, are precisely the kind of determinants which are pre-eminently important for the psychologist.

These observations are even more important today than they were when they were written. For, as Bartlett mentioned, the difficulties raised by over-emphasizing determination by the stimulus become more apparent as more highly complex responses are examined. As experimental psychology has pushed on to deal with more highly organized behaviour, this limitation has become increasingly serious. More and more variations in external circumstances are examined, but as the findings accumulate it often becomes harder, not easier, to make meaningful generalizations. In the experimental study of memory, for instance, Irion states that 'the variability of technique among experimenters is enormous . . . gratuitous variation of practically every circumstance under which learning occurs, and this without plan or design, has made it impossible to compare results that should be, at least roughly,

39

comparable'. He adds that 'this situation exists in most other areas of psychology, of course', and concludes by referring to 'the present state of relative chaos' (Irion, 1959, pp. 546–59).

But though Bartlett pointed so clearly to a major task of experimental psychology, his own work illustrated rather than solved the problem. It was clear that inner factors were operating, but they were not subjected to strict control. This has been brought out in some recent experiments by Gauld and Stephenson (1967). Bartlett had asked his subjects to reproduce, on a number of successive occasions, material which they had seen once. He concluded from the records that remembering was normally exceedingly subject to error, and suggested that memory must be regarded as an active process of construction, influenced by convention and expectation, rather than an accurate record of past events as originally presented. Gauld and Stephenson, however, have shown that subjects' records are likely to contain much *deliberate* guesswork. Subjects can distinguish, in their records, those parts which they believe to be accurate, from those parts which they believe they invented. These beliefs are substantially correct: the subject can pick out his own errors. Further, strict instructions to be accurate reduce the errors. This suggests rather strongly that the subjects in Bartlett's experiments were not doing their best to *remember*. Hence remembering in everyday life probably contains less unwitting error than Bartlett supposed. (In addition, Bartlett used much odd and unfamiliar material which would probably lend itself to the kinds of change he found.) The upshot is that, in order to support Bartlett's conclusions, it would be necessary to establish a strict control over the subject's guessing. As Gauld and Stephenson say, 'If an outstandingly conscientious person, whose errors would certainly not be the result of conscious guessing or invention, distorted prose passages despite great moral pressure to be accurate, then indeed one could start enquiring whether some basic feature of memory mechanisms were being laid bare' (Gauld and Stephenson, 1967, p. 47). As they also point out, 'So far no experiments have specifically met these conditions' (Gauld and Stephenson, 1967).

If one lesson is the extreme complexity of the inner conditions which need to be controlled, there is also a further lesson, which we have met before. Bartlett's conclusion that 'remembering is normally exceedingly subject to error' (Bartlett, 1932,

p. 176) seems likely to have been an exaggeration. Kay (1955) has also emphasized the substantial accuracy of subjects' reproductions, especially at initial recall. But Bartlett saw his conclusion as correcting a common lay misconception. He wrote, 'It looks as if what is said to be reproduced is, far more often than is commonly admitted, really a construction' (Bartlett, 1932, p. 176). But now it looks as if our ordinary experience is not, after all, a bad guide. Bartlett refers to some of his results as 'startling' (ibid., p. 175). They could, of course, only be startling if they conflicted with the expectations which we have formed on the basis of our everyday experience. But it is highly unlikely that everyday experience should lead us to form expectations about the accuracy of memory which are substantially incorrect. If we are surprised by the statement that remembering is normally exceedingly subject to error, it is because the experiments on which this conclusion is based are more limited and less reliable than ordinary experience. One wonders how many examinees have received high marks for correctly recalling that human remembering is normally exceedingly subject to error.

Bartlett's contention that inner as well as outer conditions must be considered, has often been repeated since. The point was made in a leading textbook of experimental psychology in these words (Woodworth and Schlosberg, 1954, p. 3):

> Since O [the subject or organism] certainly responds differently to different stimuli, there must be stimulus variables, S-factors, affecting the response. Just as certainly, the subject responds differently to the same identical stimulus according to his own state and intentions at the moment. There are O-variables . . . affecting the response. . . . The response depends on the stimuli acting at that moment and on factors present in the organism at that moment. This general statement can be put into the form of an equation, $R=f(S,O)$, which reads that the response is a function of S-factors and O-factors.

It might seem, then, that this point is so well known that there is no need to labour it. But there are at least two good reasons for continuing to draw attention to it. The first is that, however much the experimenter may pay lip-service to it, and agree that inner conditions are important, the exigencies of the experimental situation continually throw him back in practice to an excessive reliance on the control of outer conditions. As Zangwill, Bartlett's successor at Cambridge, remarks, experimental control of internal circumstances is 'difficult, if not impossible, to achieve' (Zangwill, 1964a, p. 134). This being so, the experimenter suffers a permanent temptation to exaggerate the importance of external circumstances. A recent example is to be found in a work on perception, edited by Welford and Houssiadas (1970). The gist of the theoretical section is summed up by Welford as follows : 'Perception is not to be understood as a matter of sensory data alone, but rather in terms of more or less elaborate constructs or frameworks' (ibid., p. 19). In our terms, inner conditions are important as well as outer. At the same time, and apparently with no awareness of the contrast, the editors refer to the experimental section as 'aimed at accounting, in terms of stimuli reaching the eye, for features of perception which are often regarded as matters of inference and judgement' (ibid., p. 3). The logic of the problem leads the theorist to stress inner activity; the limitations of psychological experiment lead the experimentalist to stress outward and controllable stimuli.

The second reason for focusing on this problem is that it is most important to try to ensure that we know why the psychologist should not stand in awe of the stimulus. This comes to the fore when we ask exactly what is involved in controlling the outer conditions.

The prime example of the tendency to stand in awe of the stimulus is, of course, the stimulus-response formula of Watson. When we ask how far outer conditions can be identified and controlled, and how far the response can be treated as a function of these outer conditions, we are asking how far the S-R formula provides a satisfactory framework for psychological explanation. (Here it might be objected that Watson included internal as well as external stimuli in his formula – for example, stomach contractions and sexual tensions as well as light and sound – and that he therefore did not place an exclusive emphasis on external conditions. The significant point, however, is that internal stimuli are comparable with external in so far as both types initiate activity at the receptor organs, and the intention of the formula is to establish systematic relations between receptor activity and response, independently of further conditions internal to the nervous system. Since sight and hearing are in any case the dominant senses, the S-R formula is commonly taken as implying that behaviour is primarily determined by outer conditions.)

For the early behaviourists, this formula seems to have held a welcome simplicity after the complexities of earlier views; and some behaviourists still write as if the formula was a perfectly straightforward matter. In fact, if one thing has become clear, from the writings of numerous critics over a long period, it is that the meaning of the terms 'stimulus' and 'response' is thoroughly ambiguous. We may approach this ambiguity by considering the definitions provided by a modern behaviourist.

In the version given by Broadbent, we find two contrasting statements. He first writes: 'If we compiled a set of laws, each of which said that when certain things are seen or heard by a man he will perform certain actions, these laws could readily be checked' (Broadbent, 1961, p. 38). Shortly afterwards, he describes psychology as 'a science which relates events at the bodily senses ["stimuli"] to events at those parts of the body which act on the outer world ["responses"]' (ibid., p. 41). But clearly there is a great difference between events at the bodily senses, and things seen or heard by a man: the former refers to the radiation impinging on the sense organs, and may be called the 'actual stimuli'; the latter refers to 'external objects'. Clearly also there is a great difference between events at those parts of the body which act on the outer world, and performing certain actions: the former refers to what may be called 'muscular contractions'; the latter refers to what is achieved through such muscular contraction, and may be called the 'external result'. What does this difference mean in practice?

In practice, experimenters often prefer to talk in terms of external objects rather than actual stimuli, and of external results rather than muscular contraction. This is how Woodworth and Schlosberg describe it (op. cit., p. 4):

In experiments on learning and problem solving no complete record is usually made of the actual stimuli received by the subject's receptors. What you find instead is a statement of the objective situation confronting the subject – a maze, for example, of specified form and size under specified illumination. The stimuli received by an animal traversing the maze could scarcely be specified since they change from moment to moment as the animal moves. Objects, not stimuli, are recorded in this case. Similarly, little attempt is made to describe the animal's motor responses or muscular contractions. Instead, you find a report of the external result of the animal's movements, such as entering a certain blind alley or passing it by. It is customary to report external objects and results in such experiments, rather than the actual stimuli and responses; and no harm is done if we recognize that two of the main problems of psychology are being by-passed, the problem of how external objects are perceived and the problem of how muscular activity is directed towards external results.

But is it wholly for the sake of convenience, as this passage seems to imply, that the experimenter prefers to talk of external objects and results, rather than actual stimuli and muscular contractions? And is no harm really done when we by-pass certain main problems, even if we recognize that we are doing so? And why should the behaviourist retain the formulation in terms of actual stimuli and muscular contractions, if in practice he is going to prefer that in terms of external objects and results? These questions are all related, and to answer them is to discover the limitations of the stimulus-response formula.

Consider first the relation between external objects and actual stimuli. There is no constant relation between a given external object and the actual stimuli which it produces. The same external object gives rise to many different actual stimuli according to variations in its distance from the organism, the state of the illumination, and so on; while different external objects may produce the same actual stimuli on different occasions. For example, an external object of a given magnitude casts retinal images of different size as its distance from the organism varies; while external objects of different magnitude may all cast retinal images of the same size if they are at appropriately different distances. Similar considerations apply to the relation between external results and muscular contractions. There is no constant relation between a given external result and the muscular contractions by which it is produced.

The same external result may be produced by many different muscular contractions on different occasions; while different external results may be produced by the same muscular contractions on different occasions. For example, the same external result, killing a man, may follow many different muscular contractions, as in throttling, stabbing or shooting; while the same muscular contraction, flexing the fore-finger, may produce different external results, as in shooting a man, a rabbit, a target, and so on.

These familiar facts have important consequences. A first consequence is that the definition of psychology as 'a science which relates events at the bodily senses ('stimuli') to events at those parts of the body which act on the outer world ('responses')' (Broadbent, 1961, p. 41) needs to be examined with great caution. Clearly any attempt to establish systematic relations between particular actual stimuli and particular muscular contractions would be both hopeless and pointless. It would be hopeless because it is inconceivable that there should be any regular correspondence between particular actual stimuli which may result from many different external objects, and particular muscular reactions which may produce many different external results. It would be pointless because, even if such regularities could be found, we should have omitted what is significant in the life of the organism. The significance of the actual stimulus lies in its relation to the external object. The significance of the muscular contraction lies in the external result which follows. Behaviour is an attempt to cope with objects and achieve results, not to correlate actual stimuli and muscular contractions. A psychology which restricted itself to relating 'events at the bodily senses to events at those parts of the body which act on the outer world' would be omitting the reasons why these events are significant for the organism. Hence this formulation is, by itself, insufficient, and it is understandable that the behaviourist should also wish to refer to external objects and external results.

There is also a further reason for introducing external objects and results. We have seen that it would be mistaken to look for systematic relations between particular actual stimuli and particular muscular contractions. The appropriate actual stimuli to consider are rather all those which may derive from a given external object; just as the appropriate muscular contractions to consider are all those which may give rise to a particular external result. It is only in considering such collections of actual stimuli and muscular contractions that it is reasonable to look for coherent and meaningful relations between events at the bodily senses and events at those parts of the body which act on the outer world, for it is these collections of stimuli and contractions which are involved when the organism tries to cope with objects and achieve results. It is here that we come to the crucial point. It is only through knowing which external object is involved, that it is possible to pick out the relevant collection of actual stimuli; and it is only through knowing what external result is involved, that it is possible to pick out the relevant collection of muscular contractions. It is only through this knowledge that it is possible to discover which collections are the candidates for entering into predictable sequences. It is for this reason also, therefore, that the experimenter must introduce external objects and results, for otherwise he would not know which events at the bodily senses to correlate with which events at those parts of the body which act on the outer world.

We have reached the conclusion that it is necessary for the behaviourist to introduce external objects and results, not merely for the sake of convenience, and not merely because this provides a more meaningful description of behaviour, but above all because it is only in this way that it is possible to know which collections of actual stimuli to correlate with which muscular contractions. It seems, then, that it is unsatisfactory to define psychology as a search for systematic relations between actual stimuli and muscular contractions: external objects and results must be introduced. This brings us to the alternative version of the S-R formula, in which we talk of external objects and external results, which as we have seen is often preferred by experimenters in practice. Will this prove satisfactory?

At first sight, this second version of the formula, in which the experimenter reports external objects and results, may seem to be a straightforward matter. The reader will recall the passage quoted from Woodworth and Schlosberg, on pp. 43–4, in which they remarked that the experimenter might give 'a statement of the objective situation confronting the subject – a maze, for example, of specified form and size under specified illumination' and also 'a report of the external result of the animal's movements, such as entering a certain blind alley or passing it by'. But in by-passing the problem of perception, this conceals a difficulty. Certainly everyone can agree on what the objective situation is, at least in cases such as this, but the experimenter is taking it for granted that he himself, as well as the subject, can perceive this situation. He is assuming the everyday understanding of the world. But the introduction of everyday understanding transforms the problem. We are no longer concerned with 'outer conditions' described simply in terms of the radiation which impinges upon the organs of sense; but with the outer world as we know it or believe it to be. We have found that it is necessary to do this, for otherwise we should have no means of knowing which collections of stimuli were to be taken as belonging together. But what are the consequences of taking this step?

Broadbent, it will be recalled, spoke of compiling a set of laws, 'each of which said that when certain things are seen or heard by a man he will perform certain actions' (op. cit., p. 38). If these words are taken in their most natural sense, it must be supposed that we are to assume that the man sees and hears external things just as we all do in daily life. We must suppose that the psychologist is looking for laws describing how a man will behave if he sees a dog or a daffodil, or hears a telephone or a tambourine. It may perhaps seem that it would be very difficult to predict how a man will behave on such occasions, and very useful to know. Let us therefore examine the situation.

To examine the situation is in effect to consider what we already know about the world, including ourselves and others, as a matter of ordinary perception and simple reflection. When people see or hear certain things there are, undoubtedly, certain actions which they often perform. Chairs are often sat on, dogs often patted, cars often driven, telephones often answered, and so on indefinitely. Is it the behaviourist's intention to convert these rough tendencies into precise scientific laws? It can hardly be so, for this simply is not possible. I do not sit in every chair I see, pat every dog, drive every car, and answer every telephone. I may not do anything; or I may do something quite different. I may paint the chair, kick the dog, wash the car, and ask some-one else to answer the phone. If this was really what the

47

behaviourist had in mind – and it was the most natural interpretation of his words – two comments are in order: first, that it
it extremely difficult to think of anything we ever see or hear
which is followed by certain actions in a regular and predictable
manner; and second, that in so far as there are certain *kinds* of
things which can be done, we are already perfectly familiar
with them (though there are probably a great many new things
which someone will one day think of doing which neither the
behaviourist nor anyone else can possibly predict).

Perhaps, however, it will be said that of course this was not
what the behaviourist had in mind. The behaviourist intends us
to take the total situation into account, not simply the perception of particular objects. It may be agreed that this improves
our powers of prediction. For example, I do not cut the lawn
every time I happen to see it; but if certain circumstances are
added – that the grass is long but not wet, that it is Saturday
afternoon, and that my wife has just refused to do it – the
likelihood is increased. There are a number of very important
limitations about such a listing of circumstances as a means to
formulating laws of behaviour: the lists would be absurdly long;
they would vary enormously from person to person; and they
would require frequent correction and amplification as our
circumstances change. The most important objection, however,
is that in so far as these circumstances do determine our
behaviour, we already know very well what they are in our own
case, and if we want to know what they are for others we can
ask them.

But even with the fullest description of the external situation,
it remains impossible usually to predict the response. This is
because we have omitted the central factor in the equation: the
person himself and what he wants to do. Even in the most
favourable external circumstances, I may not cut the lawn if I
have something more attractive to do. Unless the inner motive
is right, the behaviour is not forthcoming. You can lead the
horse to the water but you cannot make it drink.

We can now see (if, under the mystifying influence of
behaviourism, we did not already know) what information we
need to predict what actions a man will perform. We need a
comprehensive account of the present situation as the man
understands it, much information about his past experiences,
and a knowledge of his current motives and feelings. But from

the point of view of behaviourism, this information has two serious drawbacks. First, it would enable us to achieve the behaviourist's aim, but only by including all the things he wanted to leave out – the person's understanding of the world, and what he thinks and feels about it. Second, we already possess a vast quantity of this information. It is precisely this which every man already bears in mind, explicitly or implicitly, when he decides what he will do; and it is because we have it that we are properly described as self-conscious and reasonable beings, capable of predicting and controlling our own behaviour.

An example may help to tie these points together. If, as I am driving my car, I see that I am being followed by the police, I may, if I am a law-abiding citizen, reduce my speed to within the permitted limit. Alternatively, if I am making my getaway from a successful bank raid, I may accelerate to ninety. In neither case do I respond simply to particular actual stimuli, but in terms of my recognition of the meaning which those stimuli have in our culture, of my awareness of what I have been doing in the recent past, of my knowledge of the legal and social consequences of the courses of action which are open to me, and so on. What I choose to do depends upon the outcome which I want to secure, whether it is to avoid losing my licence for speeding, or to avoid losing my liberty for theft. When we understand the situation as the actor understands it, and when we understand him as he understands himself, we understand his behaviour too – as he does himself. We have answered the behaviourist's question by leaving the behaviourist behind.

It becomes abundantly plain that the phrase 'outer conditions' is thoroughly ambiguous. Each of us knows far more about the world, and his relation to it, than could possibly be given to the senses at a particular moment. In one sense, outer conditions refers to the world described simply in terms of the radiation which impinges upon the organs of sense, and in this interpretation they can be precisely controlled and identified. In another sense, the phrase refers to the world as we perceive it or believe it to be, and in this interpretation it is highly problematic whether precise definition or control is possible at all. For in this sense, 'outer conditions' depend upon the subject's activity. When we add the person's feelings, wants and interests, we see that the information required to predict behaviour lies within the organism, in precisely that area which the behaviourist wishes to omit. It is these inner conditions which lead us to perceive the environment as we do – as a world of familiar persons, objects and situations. This environment is not a set of conditions, independent of ourselves, which forces us to behave in certain ways. It is largely man-selected and man-made. It is already an expression of human needs and purposes. It is a field of opportunities for the satisfaction of human intentions, not a set of independent conditions to which we must passively submit. Behaviourism, with its stress on outer rather than inner conditions, puts the cart before the horse, misunderstands the cart, and ignores the horse.

Bartlett's theme – that the psychologist, of all people, should not stand in awe of the stimulus, and that internal conditions are pre-eminently important for him – is one which might be illustrated from the writings of many psychologists over a long period. It was to be expected, then, that the behaviourists would eventually realize that the S-R formula is incomplete, and would turn their attention to inner factors. But it is only with reluctance that they abandon that simple and beguiling equation – a reluctance which is thoroughly justified, for this marks the beginning of the end for behaviourism. Here we may note the manner in which Broadbent comes to recognize its limitations.

Broadbent (1961), as we have seen, begins by putting forward the S-R formula as the pattern of psychological explanation. But halfway through his book he has occasion to refer to the views of his fellow-behaviourist Skinner, who has always resisted the pressure to introduce inner conditions. Broadbent describes Skinner as holding the view that 'we ought simply to say what we do to the animal, what the animal does in return, and to find out regularities in the relation between these two kinds of observation' (Broadbent, 1961, p. 126). This is the view which Broadbent himself originally recommended to his readers; but now he decides that it is unsatisfactory. He writes (ibid., pp. 132 and 188):

Unfortunately, behaviour does not altogether lend itself to rules of that sort. On a simple observational level, an

animal placed in the same situation does not always do the same thing. . . . A rat, who normally responds to the sight of a runway by running eagerly along it, will not do so if he has previously been shocked in the food-box at the far end.

It is almost universally recognized now that even the behaviour of rats requires us to think of mechanisms operating purely inside their brains.

But if behaviour does not altogether lend itself to rules of that sort, it would be better not to begin by suggesting that it does. It would be better also not to depict this tardy rediscovery of the obvious as a milestone in the progress of scientific psychology, especially when so many other psychologists have been pointing it out for so long. Of most significance, however, is the manner in which Broadbent reaches this conclusion. He describes it as being 'on a simple observational level', and the kind of observation used should be carefully noted. The rat is described as having a *sight* of the *runway*, as running *eagerly* along it, and as being *shocked* in the *food-box*. The italicized words imply far more than could be given by objective observation. To speak of a *runway* and a *food-box* is to describe the objects in the environment as possessing functions which the animal can be assumed to recognize, and not simply as reflecting certain patterns of radiation to its senses. The words *sight*, *eagerly*, and *shocked* impute mental life to the animal. The rat's behaviour is being described in the same way that we ordinarily describe our own behaviour in daily life. A postman, one might say, who normally responds to the sight of a garden path by walking eagerly along it, will not do so if he has previously been bitten by the dog at the letterbox at the far end. The postman can see the garden path and the letterbox (a perception which implies a knowledge of 'outer conditions' far more complex than can be included in a description of the actual stimuli involved) and he does not want to be bitten again (a set of highly complex inner conditions). The behaviourist is not discovering a scientific explanation of animal behaviour, which will one day provide a basis for the understanding of human behaviour. He is simply interpreting animal behaviour by analogy with human behaviour, as we already understand it in everyday life. Naturally, his conclusions are often trite.

When the behaviourist overlooks these facts about our everyday understanding of the world, he is demonstrating once more the unfortunate consequences of what we have called 'the behaviourist's prejudice'. But some experimental psychologists might object that they are not all behaviourists, and that many experiments attempt to throw light on our perceptual abilities, taking into account the subject's report. My reply is that such experiments are for the most part conducted under extremely artificial and limited conditions, and that little or no opportunity is given for obtaining a full and unbiased account of the normal perceptual world. This point may be illustrated from the experiments of Michotte (1963) on the perception of causality. These experiments have been praised in the highest terms, but they prove on examination to be extremely defective (Joynson, 1971).

Basically, these experiments consist in presenting the subject with a small rectangular framework, within which he can see two small squares moving backwards and forwards in relation to each other. When certain movements, at certain speeds, are presented, the subject may receive the impression that one object is pushing or pulling the other. Michotte concludes that when certain stimulus conditions are fulfilled, within fairly narrow limits, there is a process of perceptual 'organization' which gives rise to a perception of causality. Most of his experiments then consist in exploring many variations on this theme. Now certainly this may rightly be regarded as in many ways an improvement on the behaviourist position. There is a recognition that perception involves an inner contribution, and there is an attempt to describe this perception as it seems to the observer. At the same time, it may be criticized as not departing far enough from the behaviourist point of view. This can be seen in two ways. First, the perceptual impression is seen as determined primarily by the immediate stimulus pattern, rather than by the past experience of the person, or any process of inference. Second, the treatment of the subject's reports was in many ways unsatisfactory.

From a detailed examination of Michotte's text, the writer concluded that the great majority of his experiments were in fact conducted on only a small group of subjects, numbering about half-a-dozen and mainly comprising Michotte himself and his immediate colleagues. It is rare to find that subject's reports, which actually are rather infrequent, are ascribed to any particular subject, and it is obvious that such a method is highly unreliable as a basis for generalization. So small a group would quickly establish its own preconceptions and accepted interpretations, which would naturally be those agreeable to the chief subject, Michotte. Some of the experiments were conducted on larger groups, but even some of these were carried out during lectures and demonstrations of Michotte's ideas, and there was no formal method of recording the subject's opinions. Michotte claimed that virtually all his subjects gave results in accordance with his own interpretations, but later work has often given substantially different results, suggesting a markedly greater emphasis on constructive inner activity (see Joynson, 1971).

Boyle (1972), who had worked under the direction of Michotte, has accepted the author's criticisms of Michotte's experimental methods, and adds that the influence of suggestion was 'blatant and direct'. He also suggests that these criticisms do not necessarily invalidate Michotte's contribution to psychology, and that his work must be judged on grounds other than those of experimental procedure as currently understood. This may well be so, and points to the need for evolving alternative criteria. My point in the present context is that Michotte's procedure tends to a one-sided account of perception, and in particular that it fails to provide a full and unbiased treatment of the subject's report. Attempts to do this suggest that the layman is often able to give a varied and informative description (Joynson and Newson, 1962).

Michotte's work belongs to the *Gestalt* tradition, which has been a vigorous critic of behaviourism. Yet *Gestalt* theory too places great stress on current stimulation as a determinant of response: neither approach originally attempted to provide a very elaborate account of inner activities. This common feature was noted by Hebb (1949), who in his influential *Organization of Behavior* placed greater emphasis on what he called 'autonomous central processes'. In reaching this conclusion he was, of course, providing a further variation on Bartlett's theme. Thus many lines of argument converge upon the need to include inner

E

conditions in the scheme of psychological experiment. In the next chapter we shall examine some of the techniques which are currently used for this purpose; but it must be said that we shall then, unfortunately, be in a better position to appreciate why so many experiments are mainly concerned with outer conditions, and why this bias is so hard to overcome.

4

THE BREAKDOWN OF OBJECTIVE EXPERIMENT: INNER CONDITIONS

Sooner or later, the experimenter finds that he must take inner conditions into account. In describing how to control inner conditions, or O-variables, Woodworth and Schlosberg begin with a broad hint that this may prove difficult. They write: 'we readily admit that stimuli can be controlled so far as they come from the environment, for E [the experimenter] can manage the immediate environment consisting of the experimental room and the apparatus. But how can he control the O-variables? At first thought it seems impossible' (Woodworth and Schlosberg, 1954, p. 3). However, they distinguish two broad classes of methods. In one class, the experimenter tries to observe directly what goes on in the organism. Here they mention the methods of introspection and of physiology. In the other class, the experimenter does not try to observe directly, but 'hopes to find out indirectly by varying the conditions and noting the resulting variation in response' (ibid., p. 3). They instance the control of hunger, an inner condition, by regulating the feeding schedule. The number of hours since

55

last feeding presumably exerts a control over the strength of hunger. There are also a number of other proposals to which we shall shortly refer.

Before we examine these methods for controlling inner conditions, there are two general points which need to be borne in mind. The first concerns the use of introspection and mental concepts. The emphasis which Woodworth placed upon including introspection is rather exceptional among experimentalists. A more representative treatment of introspection is that adopted by Kling and Riggs (1972) in their recent revised edition of Woodworth and Schlosberg's book. Introspection is no longer mentioned among the legitimate methods of psychology; indeed, there is only one reference to it in a work of 1,200 pages, and that in a historical context where a comparison is drawn between 'techniques for actually studying associations, as opposed to introspecting about them' (Kling and Riggs, 1972, p. 850). The position which Kling and Riggs adopt is, of course, in conformity with the objective standpoint; and since we are concerned, in this chapter, to examine the consequences of adopting the objective method, we shall not consider it further at this point. However, it cannot be too strongly emphasized that, just because a psychologist rejects introspection, it does not follow that mental concepts will not creep into his work. In this chapter, as in the previous, we shall have occasion to note how the everyday notions of mental life appear in thinly disguised form even in the most determinedly objective of writers; and how, as a consequence, what aspires to be a scientific explanation may tell us little that we did not know before.

A second point concerns the indirect methods. Here we vary the conditions, and note the resulting variation in response. In the example given, the conditions varied were environmental. We must be on the lookout for the possibility that in every case it will prove to be environmental conditions which are varied; indeed, these methods are called indirect because it is only such conditions which are varied. But if we are only varying environmental factors, this method is not fundamentally different from experiments which only purport to control outer conditions, and therefore may be expected to suffer from the same limitations. With these preliminaries, we may first consider the indirect methods.

The inner state of 'hunger' is not something which can be observed by the experimenter. It is what is sometimes called an 'intervening variable' because it is postulated as a factor which intervenes between the 'stimulus' and the 'response'. During the 1940s, behaviourists increasingly recognized that inner factors must be taken into account, and a leading feature of what came to be known as neo-behaviourism was the attempt to incorporate 'intervening variables' into their theories.

The most celebrated theory of this type was that of Hull (1943). He postulated a number of such inner states, including 'drive', of which hunger would be an instance; 'habit strength', depending on the previous repetition of an S-R connection; 'incentive', or the reward or punishment expected; and 'inhibition', covering factors which diminished the readiness for response. His intention was first to establish control over these inner states by investigating their dependence on prior external conditions (like time since last feeding, or amount of previous learning). If these could be precisely measured, one could then investigate the interaction among these 'intervening variables' to determine how they combined to determine the momentary readiness for a particular response. This approach generated an enormous amount of experimentation involving variations in prior external conditions, kinds and frequencies of reward, and so on, and the most careful efforts were devoted to the attempt to measure these postulated factors accurately. It marked the climax of the attempt to provide a rigorous and objective account of the learning process.

Some twenty years later, Koch (1959) edited an extensive work which included a lengthy review by various contributors of the outcome of these efforts. Koch's conclusion was as follows: 'The over-all tendency of the study is to call the intervening variable paradigm and much of the associated doctrine sharply into question, and to do this in almost every sense in which questioning is possible' (ibid., p. 735). Koch mentions three main groups of difficulties.

1 It is essential to this method that it should be possible to demonstrate that, at least under certain standard conditions, a particular response depends primarily upon the variations in one particular intervening variable, which in turn depends upon variations in particular independent variables. That is to say, the link between the outer independent variables, the inner

57

intervening variable, and the final performance must be capable of a precise demonstration, which could then be used as a baseline for further elaboration. There now seems little hope that this 'defining experiment' could be achieved, or that, if it could, it would be possible to generalize from the results. The major difficulty is that there are likely to be many independent variables affecting a given intervening variable. Hunger, for example, will vary not only with time since last feeding, but also with activity during the interval, presence of other animals, strength of other motives, and so on. It would be necessary to predict the interactions among these 'indicators' in a wide range of novel situations, and also the possible interactions among intervening variables themselves. The original simplicity evaporates. Even if it proved adequate for some forms of animal behaviour, the possibility that it might be extended to human behaviour becomes remote.

2 A second class of problems concerns the generality of the variables referred to in these systems. For example, three groups of subjects might be given different degrees of practice on a certain task, with the intent of establishing different degrees of 'habit strength' – an intervening variable. But 'practice' is not a simple observable independent variable. It is a general concept with strong psychological overtones. It implies more than the sheer repetition of particular responses, namely, repetition with attention to the task, with an idea of a standard of performance, and with a view to meeting those standards in the future. Unless one calls the preliminary behaviour 'practice', it has no wider significance; but if one does, it is hard to justify. We cannot tell that a person is practising simply from observing his behaviour, and if his subsequent behaviour failed to show the expected results we should conclude, quite rightly, that he had not been practising. Similar considerations apply to concepts such as 'past training', 'heredity', or 'maintenance schedule'.

3 The most fundamental criticism concerns the purpose which the doctrine was intended to achieve. It was intended to link the theoretical constructs which were found necessary – habit strength, drive, etc. – unambiguously to observable antecedent variables, and to consequent dependent variables. This provided an 'operational definition' of the constructs, and was regarded as protecting the psychologist against the introduction of vague and non-empirical notions. But as we approach

the more complex problems of personality and social psychology, the kinds of concepts which are used – repression, ego strength, role, introversion, complex – seem impossible to tie down to observable antecedents. In addition, it must always be remembered that the way the environment is perceived – as threatening, welcoming, familiar, and so on – is in effect another 'intervening variable'. Koch remarks that many theorists of the person and the social context could accept without embarrassment a view of their constructs which held that they were *all* intervening variables. Even at the level of sensory theory, the difficulty is encountered. 'There can be no doubt that one of the major convergences of this study is a vast, if at the moment variably applied pressure towards re-examination of our fundamental commitments with respect to problems of empirical definition' (Koch, 1959, p. 748; and pp. 733–49).

The limitations of this method of attempting to control inner conditions have been stated forcibly by Deese (1972). He writes (pp. 19–20):

> The heart of the experimental method . . . lies in the ability of the investigator to control some condition (independent variable) upon which some other condition (dependent variable) is said to be contingent. A change in the independent variable should be reflected in a change in the dependent variable if a contingency holds. And if the experimental method is to be useful, the link of control over the independent variable must be simple and direct. . . . It is equally important that the link between the independent and the dependent variable be simple and direct; there must be no loose linkage. This aspect of experimentation is often forgotten. If one is to apply the experimental method to the investigation of a theory in which a whole complicated pattern of intervening concepts comes between the stimulus (independent variable) and the response (dependent variable), the theory must be one for which something other than guessing and surmising provide the evidence.
>
> In psychological theory there is no established way of specifying all the subtle and intricate links that are said to exist between independent and dependent variables.

This puts in a nutshell one weakness of this method of attempting to identify and control inner factors; in strict terms, the experimenters do not know what they are talking about.

Another aspect of the method is also touched on by Deese when he remarks that 'Intervening variables were often ... familiar notions from everyday psychology – habit, attention, expectation' (1972, p. 18). This is a crucial point. It might have been supposed that these scientific theories, purporting to employ objective concepts, would have come up with something new. In fact, it is clear that these notions, and others such as 'drive' and 'incentive', are thinly disguised borrowings from the layman's everyday understanding. Again, the term 'inhibition' covers much the same ground as the familiar word 'fatigue'. Thus what purports to be an objective investigation, employing the mechanical categories of natural science, is really deriving its explanatory concepts from the language of everyday discourse, and such substance as these explanations seem to have is due to the tacit use of mentalistic terms. What is really required is an analysis of these psychological concepts, with a view to determining the kind of theory to which they are appropriate (see Charles Taylor, 1964).

It is not surprising, in view of these deficiencies of the method, that it has proved impossible to secure a clear-cut decision among the various theories of learning which have been suggested; and in reaction against this failure there seems to have been a tendency to turn away from questions about basic processes, and concentrate on the collection of experimental data in what Bitterman (1967) calls 'the new empiricism'.

A second approach to the problem of controlling inner conditions comes from the study of individual differences. Under identical outer conditions, different subjects often react differently. Clearly such differences in reaction must be due to inner differences among the subjects, which may form a permanent feature of their nature, and one long-established tradition in psychology tries to find systematic order in these individual variations. Already at the end of the last century, the first 'mental tests' were being applied, and the first statistical techniques for analysing the results were being developed. Today there is a vast array of tests, covering temperament as well as talents, and confident claims are made for the scientific character of the diagnosis. Some even assert that the major dimensions of personality can now be defined and measured. This 'psychometric' tradition has continued in rather marked separation from the experimental tradition, and what Cronbach (1957) calls the 'two disciplines' of scientific psychology have often criticized each other. The detached observer may well feel that he can agree with both.

The psychometrist has a powerful point when he argues that experimentalists too often ignore individual differences among their subjects, which are responsible for otherwise inexplicable variations from one subject to the next. Thus Eysenck (1966, p. 2) writes: 'I would like to suggest that the root of many of the difficulties and disappointments found in psychological research, as well as the cause of the well-known difficulties in duplicating results . . . lies in this neglect of individual differences.' Eysenck points to specific cases where he considers that this neglect has been wasteful, in animal as well as human psychology; and with respect to a central controversy in animal learning, that between Hull and Tolman, he suggests that differences in the strains of rats used was a major factor in confusing the issue. He writes: 'Hundreds of extremely able psychologists spent time, energy, and a considerable amount of money . . . apparently quite pointlessly; must this sort of thing be repeated endlessly before we learn the lesson that individual differences . . . may not be pushed aside and forgotten when experiments are designed which purport to reveal universal truths?' (Eysenck, 1966, p. 26).

One can entirely endorse Eysenck's protest. It is, after all, exactly that which Bartlett made forty years ago, as we have already seen. But whether the psychometric claim is justified, that these matters have now been placed on an objective scientific basis, is another question. We may first note (and this is a point which Eysenck stresses) that the practical problems would be acute. If one included only three major 'dimensions' – for example, intelligence, neuroticism and extraversion – and used only subjects who scored high, medium or low in each, one would still require to fill twenty-seven different categories. Ten subjects, say, in each category would bring the total to 270 subjects, and a very much larger number would in all probability need to be examined in order to fill the unusual categories. It would ease the experimenter's task if he could assemble a permanent panel for use on numerous occasions, but then he would face the difficult problem of possible practice effects from one experiment to the next. Altogether, this is a daunting task, however necessary it may be.

Even if these practical difficulties could be surmounted, there remain serious doubts about whether the tools available can do the job. There are two main groups of questions. The first group concerns the reliability of the testing instruments, especially in the field of personality. P. E. Vernon (1964, pp. 185–200) has examined the correlations which Eysenck has obtained on different occasions using the same tests, and finds marked variation. He concludes (1964, p. 192):

> There would seem to be an entire lack of consistency between different investigations, using somewhat different samples, both in the tests that come out as the best measures of a neuroticism factor, and in those which effectively differentiate patients from non-neurotics. These results have not been picked out as extreme ones. They are fairly typical of what happens in the personality field. Variations between the results of different authors are likely to be greater still.

The reader will also recall Vernon's doubt, referred to in the first chapter, as to whether these methods 'are consistently more accurate than the unsophisticated methods that we ordinarily use in understanding people in daily life' (ibid., p. vii).

The second group of questions concerns the statistical methods of treating test scores, known as factor analysis. The object of these methods is to deduce, from the observed pattern of correlations among the various tests, the underlying dimensions of variation among the subjects. There is a voluminous literature on the competing claims of different methods of analysis, but here we may restrict ourselves to the outcome, for it is the lack of agreement among different investigators with respect to their conclusions which finally induces scepticism. With regard to the nature of intelligence, there is a marked contrast between the British tradition, stemming from Spearman, which postulates a 'general factor' running through all intellectual performances, and the American tradition, stemming from Thurstone, which supposes that there are 'multiple factors' combining differently on different occasions. In the field of personality, the conclusions are still more varied. There are well-known divergences between the complex schemes put forward by Cattell, and the simpler systems favoured by Eysenck; and it is notable that the contrasts are not merely concerning detail, but extend to the most broad and fundamental questions. Thus whereas Eysenck is confident that introversion-extraversion has been reliably disentangled as a major dimension of variation, there is also the alternative system of Sheldon which involves a three-fold rather than two-fold classification. Sheldon's 'cerebrotonic' character corresponds roughly to Eysenck's 'introvert', but Sheldon divides Eysenck's 'extravert' character between a sociable 'viscerotonic' and a dominating 'somatotonic'. This is a disagreement which has persisted for the past twenty-five years. Thus in the field of personality, just as in that of learning, the supposedly objective methods have failed to decide among competing interpretations.

Experimentalists, aware of these and other weaknesses in the psychometric approach, are often reluctant to interest themselves in individual differences; yet this, as Eysenck indicates, is to ignore a major problem in psychological experiment, and it is not clear that experimentalists can offer any superior way of identifying inner conditions. Indeed, as we may note in conclusion, there are certain limitations which are shared by the psychometric method and that of intervening variables. First, both are attempting to identify inner conditions of response on the basis of observation of outer conditions and responses alone, whether the responses are to mental tests or to experimental situations. In neither case is the inner condition directly observed, and the inference depends upon an altogether too tenuous and indirect link. Second, as many critics have pointed out, the theorist often finishes by giving a subjectively meaningful label based upon his own view of what the tests involve, so that mentalistic description once again creeps in. The whole matter was summarized by Loevinger (1951, p. 566) in a crisp comment: 'All this computational labour – and it is usually a lot – to obtain intuitive names for hypothetical factors of mind.'

A third indirect method, which will be briefly discussed, is that which approaches behaviour from the standpoint of the theory of machines. The idea of regarding living beings as machines is a very old one, far older than that 'automaton-theory' which

James attacked, and it has always held a fascination for the scientist with his preference for mechanical explanation. For a long period, this approach was handicapped by the inability of the existing inventions to copy many of the most distinctive human performances, such as memory, problem-solving and purposive behaviour. But more recently there have been great advances in the design of machines which might be suited to this comparison, especially with respect to automatic control devices; and principles derived from cybernetics and information theory have been widely applied to psychological problems. This has certainly suggested new ways of looking at certain features of behaviour, such as thresholds and the control of certain simple movements; though not all physiologists have been impressed by the novelty or utility of the principles in relation to the nervous system. How far particular functions can be plausibly explained in this way remains highly controversial, even in relatively simple cases (see Gauld, 1966).

For our present purposes, however, the main question concerns the relation of this approach to the method of objective experiment. It can hardly be denied that it has no more achieved a means of directly controlling and identifying inner conditions, than have the other methods we have already considered. The experimenter can only conduct 'input-output' experiments, and make a more or less plausible inference as to the nature of the general system of control. He may then present us with a block diagram, with a neatly sketched indication of filters, short and long term memory stores, feedback loops, and other quasi-mechanical functions; but as far as experimental control is concerned, he is in exactly the same position as those who prefer to imagine intervening variables or statistical factors. The link of control is equally tenuous, and the possibility of distinguishing among competing hypotheses is just as remote. So far as experimental technique is concerned, we are still restricted to the control of outer conditions with all the limitations which that implies.

But so far as choice of hypotheses is concerned, this method seems to be very much more limited than the others. They were based mainly upon the observation of behaviour or upon the results of mental tests, but these depend largely upon what happens to be available in current machine theory – developed, it must always be remembered, in a different context. Hence there is a tendency to deny behavioural characteristics for which no mechanical analogy is currently available. In the days before cybernetics, 'purpose' was a forbidden concept. With the arrival of 'feedback', it is re-admitted, with the implication that a scientific explanation is now available; though this is, in reality, a highly complex problem in conceptual analysis (see Charles Taylor, 1964). It is hardly too much to suggest that, instead of behaviour being examined to decide what mechanical hypothesis, if any, is appropriate, machine theory is examined to decide what behaviour is acceptable.

It is hardly surprising that to many experimentalists this approach seems altogether too speculative, and that, when they recall that the interval between the stimulus and the response is occupied by the nervous system, they wish to tackle the problem more directly. Weiskrantz (1964, p. 49) writes:

If one is interested in the brain, rather than a hypothetical model, this approach may be illusorily simple. The history of the 'conceptual' nervous system, from Erasistratus, through Galen, Descartes and the stimulus-response psychology, is a very lengthy one, ante-dating even the history of its principal laboratory tool, the armchair.

We have considered three main ways of attempting to find out what goes on between the stimulus and the response, all of which may be classified as indirect. In the phrase of Woodworth and Schlosberg, the experimenter 'hopes to find out indirectly by varying the conditions and noting the resulting variation in response'. But so far as experimental control is concerned, these are really versions of the stimulus-determination position, for it is only outer conditions which they can observe and control. Thus these methods suffer the ambiguity with respect to the definition of outer conditions which we have already noted: namely, that this definition may assume the perceptual capacities of the observer, instead of restricting itself to a purely objective account. In addition, these methods have weaknesses of their own. First, the link of control over the supposed inner conditions is far too loose to satisfy the stringent requirements of experimental precision; and second the description of these factors frequently betrays its origin in the mental concepts of everyday life. It is not surprising that these methods fail to

65

decide among competing hypotheses, and it becomes plain that the experimenter must attempt to come to terms with inner conditions in some more straightforward way.

This brings us to the direct methods mentioned by Woodworth and Schlosberg. From the strict objective standpoint, introspection is inadmissible; and since we are assessing the method of objective experiment, introspection cannot be considered as a possible method in this context. The only remaining possibility is the method of physiological investigation. From the objective standpoint this is, indeed, the obvious way. The gap between sense organ and muscle is occupied, after all, by the nervous system. Surely, then, this is what the experimentalist should be studying. The logic of this conclusion is so strong that it becomes an interesting question, why so many experimentalists, though holding the most impeccably objective principles, nevertheless fail to act upon it, and instead follow the unsatisfactory paths we have so far examined. The answer is, of course, that this final method has its own drawbacks, and it is these which drive many experimentalists back to the indirect methods.

A first limitation is simply that knowledge of higher nervous function is at present severely restricted. We do not know, for example, what changes if any take place in the nervous system during learning, and with respect to most of the more complex forms of behaviour we know little or nothing about the actual mechanisms which might be involved, as distinct from the parts of the brain where they may be localized. Some writers have also doubted whether contemporary techniques are likely to throw much light on the function of the brain as a whole (Gregory, 1961). Nevertheless, over the past century, impressive progress has been made. It is here that psychology comes into the closest relations with the natural sciences, and here too that the perennial problem of mind and body comes to its sharpest focus. Indeed, so many problems of the greatest interest are raised in this area, that it is hard to sympathize with those behaviourists who have deprecated attention to it and preferred to explore the indirect methods. However, when we ask why they have adopted this attitude, we come to a second problem which this approach presents.

This second question concerns the proper relationship between psychology and physiology. Watson himself thought it important to distinguish behaviourism from physiology, and anticipated that his readers might raise the question. He wrote: 'Indeed you may wonder, as we proceed, whether behaviourism can be differentiated from that science' (1924b, p. 11). His answer was that physiology 'is particularly interested in the functioning of the parts of the animal . . . behaviourism . . . is intrinsically interested in what the whole animal will do' (ibid.). This conception has served for a long period to satisfy inquirers, and is still often used today. It gives to psychology the task of formulating S-R relationships, and to physiology the task of discovering the actual neural connections. Thus behaviourists have been opposed to overmuch 'neurologizing', in part at least because they believed that behavioural explanation should remain at the behavioural level, thus preserving a distinctive role for psychology and leaving physiological explanation to physiology. For this view, there was of course no problem of relating mental life and brain action, for mental life had given place to behaviour.

But this mode of conceiving the relation of psychology and physiology seems now to be breaking down, and this for at least two good reasons. The first is that the original S-R formula is gradually receding; and as the importance of inner conditions is increasingly recognized, it becomes plain that physiological mechanisms must play a more fundamental role in an objective explanation. They can no longer be regarded as providing a kind of supplementary explanation, which could be added by another science after the laws of behaviour had been established. They must be seen as a necessary part of the conditions determining behaviour, so that physiological investigation becomes an integral part of objective experiment.

The second reason for the breakdown of this way of conceiving the relation is that it entails an inadequate idea of the scope of physiology. It is certainly true that there are many occasions when the physiologist is primarily interested in parts of the body studied in relative isolation, as with respiration, circulation and digestion (though even here the physiologist will always have in mind the role which these functions play in the whole bodily economy). But the neurophysiologist, by contrast, is primarily interested in the nervous system precisely because it co-ordinates bodily activity as a whole. Thus Sherrington wrote (1947, p. 2):

67

In the multicellular animal, especially for those higher reactions which constitute its behaviour as a social unit in the natural economy, it is nervous reaction which *par excellence* integrates it, welds it together from its components, and constitutes it from a mere collection of organs an animal individual.

Thus the contrast which Watson drew between psychology and physiology does not hold, and the physiological psychologist is interested in the nervous system precisely because it has this integrating function.

The convergence of these two trends seems to point inescapably to the conclusion that, from the standpoint of objective science, the explanation of behaviour must be sought in the study of the brain. The conclusion is, indeed, one which many psychologists accept, and which seems to be clearly expressed by Zangwill when he writes: 'It is indeed not too much to suggest that the neurology of today may well provide the psychology of tomorrow with its basic principles' (Zangwill, 1964a, p. 130); and also when he states that 'the ultimate aim of psychology is to establish a system of general laws covering the whole field of higher nervous activity' (Zangwill, 1967, p. 294).

But what now becomes of the relation between psychology and physiology? Clearly this view marks the end of the behaviourist belief that psychology seeks laws of behaviour independently of physiology, for now it is neurology which is to provide the basic principles. It marks the end of the attempt which the behaviourists and others have made to distinguish the spheres of psychology and neurology, and instead sees them as merging. Thus Zangwill (1964b) expresses a hope that 'a coalescence of neurology and psychology may ultimately be achieved'. This is the conception of 'neuropsychology', which seeks principles which are common to psychology and neurology, and hopes that 'as understanding of the brain conceived as the instrument of behaviour advances, both neurology and psychology will become increasingly integrated into a single scientific discipline' (Zangwill, 1971, p. 89).

There are many points which remain obscure in this conception, not least the meaning of the phrase 'the brain as the instrument of behaviour'. The difficulties centre on the role which the psychologist is supposed to play. There is no mention of mental life, so we cannot say that psychology is concerned with mind or psyche, as did Sherrington and the earlier dualists. On the other hand, we cannot say that psychology seeks laws of behaviour of the kind that Watson envisaged, independently of physiology. Thus the whole earlier attempt to find a distinctive sphere for psychology, whether on behaviourist or on dualist lines, seems to have been abandoned. If the only valid principles derive from neurology, it is not clear what the psychologist has to contribute, or what the word 'psychology' stands for in the term 'neuropsychology'.

It cannot be too strongly emphasized that 'neuropsychology' is an attempt to indicate the sphere of psychology as such. It is not an attempt to indicate the aims of some one area of psychology, which might co-exist with other areas, in the way that in the past physiological psychology has been thought of as one area along with others such as social, or comparative, or differential. Indeed, it is not clear how these other areas of psychology can find a place, unless neurological principles are forthcoming to explain their findings. Zangwill (1971) denies that his view implies a 'takeover' by neurology, or that psychology as we know it today will simply cease to exist. But such statements need to be explained and justified. A great deal of current psychology is remote from neurology, and is likely to remain so for a long time to come. Indeed, there are some who believe 'that some aspects of behaviour can never be dealt with in neurological terms alone' (Hebb, 1972a, p. 278). But what is the status of such areas? If they are capable of finding valid principles independently of neurology, we have departed from the standpoint of neuropsychology (and the nature of these principles requires explanation). If, however, they are not capable of finding valid principles independently of neurology, it is not clear why, from the standpoint of neuropsychology, they should continue to exist.

The stimulus-response formula attempted to provide a form of explanation which on the one hand enabled the psychologist to avoid falling back upon the categories of mental life, and on the other hand enabled him to distinguish his sphere from that of the physiologist. With the collapse of behaviourism – first in the simple S-R version, and then in the intervening-variable form – the scientific psychologist once again finds himself confronted with a choice between mentalistic and physiological

F

explanation. He must find a new formulation of his aims and methods. An open return to mental life is unthinkable. But one cannot simply describe oneself as a neurologist. By a well-known psychoanalytic mechanism, the term 'neuropsychology' emerges as a respectable compromise-formation to resolve the conflict. But one should not inquire too closely here into the meaning of the word 'psychology'.

'What people do can be observed by others', writes Hebb (1972a, p. 13), 'and so agreement concerning the facts is possible at least in principle.' This is the heart of the behaviour-ist position, and of that method of objective experiment which was to place psychology at last upon a scientific foundation. At first, no doubt, it seemed a plain, straightforward view, but today it is coming to seem a more and more questionable doctrine.

Our questions are provoked initially by the continued failure of the method to achieve the results which were so confidently expected. Even those who remain convinced of the importance of experiment will sometimes concede that it has a long way to travel. Thus Zangwill writes that 'Experimental psychology has produced many facts, a few generalizations, and even an occasional "law". But it has so far failed to produce anything resembling a coherent and generally accepted body of scientific theory' (1964a, p. 138). Under these circumstances, it becomes inevitable that the method itself should be subjected to criticism, rather than that we should continue indefinitely to hope that it will one day bring results.

Hebb defines behaviour as 'the publicly observable activity of muscle or glands of external secretion, as manifested for example in movements of parts of the body or the appearance of tears, sweat, saliva and so forth' (1972a, p. 15). In this sense – the sense of 'muscular contraction' – it may be agreed that we can observe what people do. Similarly, we can observe, at least in principle, the 'actual stimuli' which precede these muscular contractions, and the intervening nervous activity. Here, then, there is a sequence of physical and physiological events which is open to scientific investigation. But from the point of view of psychology there is a double difficulty here. The first is that another science – physiology – has already pre-empted these events as its own field; and the second is that, as almost everyone feels, these events do not seem to characterize adequately the subject matter of psychology.

Almost all psychologists have talked as if something more was involved than this sequence of events as it may be studied from the standpoint of physiology. This is obvious in the case of a mentalistic psychologist. But it is also true of the behaviourist, for he introduces external objects and results, and eventually intervening variables as well, and uses covert mentalistic concepts in describing them. Even the neuropsychologist, by retaining the word psychology, seems to imply that he is concerned with something other than plain neurophysiology. But it is this something extra which seems to elude the precise definition and control of the experimental situation.

To the layman, it is obvious what is missed out on the objective scheme. It is the experiencing person himself, with his understanding of himself and others, who is the proper subject of psychology. And so the behaviourist revolution is complete: we are back where we started.

5
THE RETURN OF MIND

Even at the height of the influence of behaviourism, the conception of mental life was never entirely lost to view by psychology in general. It was particularly galling to behaviourists that psychoanalysis, which continued to use a mentalistic terminology and which owed nothing to experiment, should still contrive to make so dramatic an impact on the world at large. Again, there were many writers in the field of personality, from Stern to Allport, who successfully maintained a broad interest in what Bartlett called 'all that mass of determining factors which go under the names of temperament and character' and which 'are pre-eminently important for the psychologist' (1932, p. 10). The behaviourist might dismiss all such work as 'unscientific'. He could not so easily ignore all those tendencies in experimental psychology itself which refused to accept the exclusively objective approach. *Gestalt* psychology, with its stress on phenomenological observation, provided the strongest challenge, but there were also individual experimentalists, such as Woodworth or Bartlett, for whom introspection or consciousness retained a central significance. The behaviourist could hope that what was valuable in these alternatives would one day be incorporated in his own framework, but their persistence during the thirties and forties was a permanent reminder that psychology as a whole had yet to accept the leadership of behaviourism.

During the past decade, it has become increasingly clear that psychology is searching for a valid alternative to behaviourism. Powerful objections have been raised against it both in Europe and America. Burt (1962) found behaviourism 'hopelessly inadequate', and 'the need to reintroduce the concept of consciousness seems inescapable'. Koch (1964, p. 20) described the history of behaviourism as 'the gradual attenuation of a position that was never *seriously* tenable, never consistent, based on thin and shifting rationales, and adopted more to serve needs for comfort and security than a passion for knowledge'. By the mid-1960s, Mace could remark: 'Behaviourism, it would seem, is on the way out. Psychology is regaining consciousness' (1965, p. 21). But the departure of behaviourism is not something which has been marked by a final and drastic refutation. It could not be so marked, for it has not produced a clear and generally accepted theory which is open to refutation. Its essence lies in its method, and its departure consists in the slow realization that this method has not produced the results which were expected, and the gradual erosion of the belief that it ever will.

It is not too difficult for the behaviourist to shrug such opposition aside. The critic, he may say, is either a defector who could not stand the heat in the kitchen, or he is an outsider who somehow escaped the benefits of a behaviourist education. What the behaviourist cannot ignore, however, is the remarkable shifts of standpoint which are occurring among leading figures in the behaviourist camp itself. Koch has referred to what he aptly calls 'the return of the repressed', by which he means 'the massive return to a concern with empirical problem areas long bypassed or only glancingly acknowledged because of their subjectivist "odor" [or, I would add, because of an entirely realistic appraisal of the difficulties of significant progress on these problems in an exclusively "objective" mode]' (1964, p. 19). The areas he mentions are perception, language behaviour, thinking, and so-called mediational processes in general. To this we may add that not only are these areas coming back into fashion, but behaviourists are showing a marked tendency to describe and discuss them in mentalistic terms at the same time that they maintain that they have not abandoned their objective principles. We shall next examine some examples of this final stage of behaviourism, in which the behaviourist uses the concepts of mental life, and uses them in their proper original meaning as referring to subjective experience, and yet tries to persuade himself that this total defeat may be portrayed as the final victory of Watson's great endeavour. And as Koch remarks: 'When the ludicrousness of the position is made sufficiently plain, perhaps it will be laughed out of existence' (1964, p. 20).

We have seen that some objective psychologists import mental concepts without realizing what they are doing. We come now to some who do so deliberately, yet vigorously insist that they are merely completing the behaviourist programme. This is a delicate operation, and Watson was fortunate that he did not live long enough to endure the triumph.

We have already noticed Hebb's argument that both behaviourism and *Gestalt* theory postulate too rapid a transition from sensory stimulus to motor response, and that the interval is frequently occupied with what the layman calls thinking, and the psychologist calls 'autonomous central process' (Hebb, 1949). Somewhat later, Hebb suggested that to deal adequately with this interval a 'second phase' was needed in the psychological revolution. 'In the psychological revolution,' he wrote, 'the second phase is just now getting under way. The first banished thought, imagery, volition, attention, and other such seditious notions. . . . It is the task of the second phase to bring them back, brainwashed as necessary' (Hebb, 1960, p. 736). This is termed 'behaviouristics'.

In his most recent exposition of his standpoint, Hebb (1972a) begins by describing psychology as the study of the mind. But if anyone supposed that Hebb had strayed inadvertently into the nineteenth century, and wished to advocate the study of a subjective activity, known through introspection and contrasted with bodily process, he is quickly corrected. Hebb stops any such back-sliding by asserting at once that mind, even one's own mind, is not open to inspection. Introspection, he writes, 'does not exist' (Hebb, 1972a, p. 2). It is only through inference from behaviour that we can acquire knowledge of mind.

Further, what we then infer is not something immaterial – a non-physiological controlling agent – but 'a bodily activity, the activity of the brain or some part of that activity' (ibid., p. 4). This is indeed only a working hypothesis, but the psychologist proceeds, apparently, on the assumption that everything is to be explained in physiological terms. In the remainder of the book, Hebb makes free use of mentalistic terms such as sensation and perception, but we soon discover what is meant by brain-washing seditious notions. They are all carefully defined in physiological terms (ibid., glossary, pp. 293ff). Sensation means 'activity of receptors and specific afferent pathways', not a subjective experience; perception means 'activity of mediating processess', not an awareness of the existence and nature of external objects (and a mediating process is described as 'an activity of the brain'); knowledge means 'some modification of central processes', and 'central processes' turn out to be 'an activity within the CNS' (central nervous system). There is nothing in this to which the most puritanical behaviourist could object.

But we are left with a troublesome question. If this is what you mean by 'mind', and by these other old-fashioned words, why use them? What conceivable purpose is served by using terms, which the student is bound to understand initially in a mentalistic sense, if you must straightway explain that you do not intend them to be taken in this way? It might be suggested, perhaps, that the object is to ensure that the student, who might otherwise spontaneously introduce these words in their natural sense, will in future only use them in what is regarded as a proper scientific sense. But it is illegitimate to attempt to establish one's point of view, by taking words which have a commonly accepted sense which runs counter to that point of view, and insisting that they be used in another sense consistent with it. This is simply to deprive those who disagree with you, of the language in which they could express their disagreement. The behaviourist who adopts this procedure should ask himself how he would react if a mentalist said: 'Psychology studies the activity of the brain, but please remember that when I say "brain" I mean, not a bodily process, but an immaterial agent.'

But it is at the end of Hebb's book that we discover, I think, the crucial reason for re-introducing mentalistic terms. There we find that the need arises through what Hebb calls 'the necessary limitations of neurologizing' (ibid., p. 278). Even the simplest behaviour of the whole organism involves the activity of enormous numbers of nerve cells, and it is impossible to record all this in detail. Instead, one uses neurological constructs such as 'volley of impulses' or 'level of firing'. 'But the intricacies of brain function are such that this still does not take us far enough, and we reach a point at which the use of psychological conceptions, on a still larger scale of complexity, becomes inevitable' (ibid., p. 278). In other words, 'psychological constructs' are introduced when and because 'neurological constructs' are inadequate. 'It seems,' writes Hebb, 'that some aspects of behavior can never be dealt with in neurological terms alone' (ibid., p. 278). This undermines the conception of 'neuropsychology' and Hebb's own starting-point as well. For *originally* Hebb stated that the inference from behaviour to mind is an inference to 'the activity of the brain'; *now* we find that the inference is made precisely where we do not know what the brain activity is, and where it seems unlikely that we shall ever know completely. But if Hebb is unable to say what these 'psychological conceptions' mean in neural terms, what does he mean by them? The answer can only be that he is using them in fundamentally the same way as any old-fashioned dualist, and that the attempt to 'brainwash' them has not worked, even for himself. We are not surprised to find that Hebb's description of one psychological construct – 'hunger' – includes 'ideas of getting and eating food'; or that his description of another – 'expectancy' – includes 'anticipatory imagery or ideation'. It seemed at first that Hebb was re-introducing mental terms, but defining them physiologically, simply in order to teach the student to think scientifically. But now a further possibility occurs. Is it not possible that the function of these new linguistic conventions is to conceal from Hebb himself the fact that he is really thinking in mentalistic terms, and to enable him to believe that he remains a true behaviourist when he is actually a crypto-dualist? The 'seditious notions' have not been brainwashed: they have only been whitewashed.

Two considerations lend support to this conclusion. The first concerns a comment recently made by Hebb on an article in which the writer advocated the return of mind (Joynson, 1972). Hebb (1972b) expressed 'astonishment' at the 'idea that the mind has been lost in objective psychology', and assured us that he and other objective psychologists are concerned to study 'the mind'. But no one could reasonably suppose that the mind had been lost in objective psychology, except in the sense of that immaterial mind which Watson rejected; nor can there be any point in assuring us that objective psychologists study the mind, unless they study it in substantially that same traditional sense. Nor could Hebb have been in any doubt that it was in this sense that I was advocating its return, for there would have been no point in advocating its return in any other sense. When, therefore, Hebb expresses 'astonishment' at the idea that mind has been lost, and assures us that he studies it, he can only be tacitly assuming that the word is to be understood in its original and common use. This shows that it is dangerous to take common words, and give them an uncommon meaning, because it may prove in the end that the reason why you chose that particular common word – as a fit subject for an uncommon meaning – was simply that it came closer than any other word to the meaning which you really wanted to express.

But this argument, it may be suggested, involves an unreliable inference from Hebb's behaviour to his state of mind, and provides inadequate evidence for the conclusion that he is really a crypto-dualist. This may be agreed. As Stout said, the inference from behaviour to mind is secondary and derivative, and must ultimately rest upon the evidence of introspection. It would be more satisfactory, therefore, if the inference from behaviour to mind, which Hebb himself advocates, could be confirmed by his own direct report of what is passing in his mind. As it happens, this is available, and provides our second line of evidence. Hebb himself, in the paper referred to above, describes his views as forming what he calls a 'protective coloring of 'pseudo-behaviorism' (Hebb, 1960). This seems an apt description of his position. It also illustrates that the simple, obvious, and generally accepted way of discovering what a man is thinking is after all the best, namely, that he should tell us what it is himself.

There remains a serious difficulty. It is certainly satisfactory from the introspective standpoint to accept Hebb's testimony in this matter, but it is not clear how Hebb, from his standpoint, can accept it himself. From his point of view, knowledge of what passes in someone's mind, even one's own, is never direct but always an inference from behaviour, either that of others or of oneself. But to assert that certain behaviour is a 'protective coloring' is to claim that, although this behaviour can usually be taken as implying a certain state of mind, nevertheless in this case it does not imply this state, but another state. But it is impossible to establish this possibility if one is restricted to making inferences from behaviour, for the only evidence one has is this behaviour, and this by definition implies the usual state of mind. From his own standpoint, therefore, Hebb cannot accept his statement that he is adopting a 'protective coloring', for he is unable to perceive what is passing in his mind. His situation is awkward. Others can accept his testimony, and know what he is thinking; but he cannot know what he is thinking himself.

Hebb could be rescued from this difficulty if he could be persuaded that introspection is possible. He supports his denial of the possibility by stating that Humphrey (1951) and Boring (1953) have denied it earlier (Hebb, 1972b). Actually, I can find no such denial in Humphrey (1951); while in his Oxford Inaugural Lecture, Humphrey (1949) writes: 'There are certain psychological problems which can at present be investigated only by the well-tried method of introspection.' Perhaps this is a case in point. Boring (1953) certainly suggests that some forms of introspection are 'not viable', but he also suggests that what he calls 'camouflaged introspection' is 'still with us, doing its business under various aliases'. Boring adds (1953, p. 186):

> The modern equivalent of introspection persists in the reports of sensory experience in psychophysics, in the protocols of patients with psychological difficulties, in the phenomenological descriptions of perception and other psychological events as provided notably by Gestalt psychologists, and also in a great deal of social psychology and psychological philosophy where the Cartesian dualism is still found to be convenient.

It does not seem, then, that Hebb's reasons for denying introspection are very sound. It may be that 'camouflaged introspection' will appeal to those who seek 'protective coloring'. But it would be wiser to dispense with these devices, for nothing makes a man look so conspicuous, as the belief that he is concealing something when everyone else can see what it is.

Some recent comments by another leading behaviourist, J. G. Taylor, provide an interesting comparison with the views of Hebb. Replying to some criticisms of objective psychology by the present writer (Joynson, 1970), J. G. Taylor (1971, p. 125) wrote: 'Psychologists, and above all behaviourists, must restore conscious experience to its rightful place as a legitimate area of research. . . . A behaviourism that persists in neglecting this important sector of behaviour might as well sink into the limbo of forgotten theories.' It seemed to me that J. G. Taylor was right to urge the restoration of conscious experience, but I doubted whether he could still legitimately call himself a behaviourist: 'It is confusing to call yourself a behaviourist when your message is the opposite of that of Watson. If that is the conclusion which you want to reach, it would be simpler to begin somewhere else' (Joynson, 1972, p. 4). In a further reply J. G. Taylor (1972) suggests that I am implying that the essence of behaviourism is the denial of consciousness, whereas it is in fact the denial of psychophysical dualism. Watson, he writes, 'excluded the language of consciousness because it appeared to be indissolubly linked to dualism'. Thus he implies that so long as he rejects dualism, he is entitled to call himself a behaviourist. But the essence of behaviourism lies in the rejection of dualism through the substitution of behaviour for consciousness: Watson regarded consciousness and dualism as indissolubly linked, and therefore rejected them together. If today one wishes to restore consciousness without restoring dualism, this may be defensible. But this is not the behaviourist way of rejecting dualism, for this is to deny the distinctive behaviourist contention that behaviour can provide a substitute for consciousness. J. G. Taylor is loosening the meaning of the word 'behaviourism' in order to go on calling himself a behaviourist, even though he has abandoned Watson's distinctive belief; and in doing so he conceals the collapse of that belief. His position can only cause confusion, for it would leave us all in doubt, when a man called himself a behaviourist, whether he was urging us to reject consciousness or imploring us to restore it.

The modern behaviourist finds himself in an increasingly untenable position. He finds it desirable, indeed essential, to refer to 'psychological conceptions', to 'the mind', to 'consciousness', and to many other things which were once the stock-in-trade of the psychology of mental life, and which

79

Watson rejected with such plain uncompromising vehemence. How can one undo the effects of his revolution, yet claim to complete it? It is tempting to re-interpret the founder's words, or suggest that he did not really mean what he said. Thus Hebb, after saying that Watson asserted 'that mind and consciousness and thought do not really exist', adds 'It is known that in some of this Watson was intentionally overstating his case, but some of it he meant' (Hebb, 1972a, p. 272). How do we know this? Is there some published statement by Watson indicating that there were parts of his doctrine which he did not mean; or indicating which parts he intended us to believe, though he did not believe them himself? Attempts to re-interpret Watson's views are likely to have the opposite of the intended effect: instead of persuading us that current 'behaviourism' is close to the original, they are more likely to convince us that the connection has finally been severed.

Lastly, one of Watson's main reasons for rejecting consciousness was its inaccessibility to objective observation. J. G. Taylor recognizes this when he states that consciousness is 'a property . . . that cannot be investigated by the ordinary objective means' (1971, p. 125). He now advocates 'the restoration of subjective reports' (1972), but he forgets to derive this from Watson's writings. It is an ironic commentary on the confusion into which behaviourists have fallen, that Taylor's plea for the restoration of subjective reports should appear in the same journal and on the very next page to Hebb's assertion that 'introspection is an illusion' (Hebb, 1972b). The next step in the argument is presumably to state that introspection – that is 'direct observation of one's own mental processes' (Hebb, 1972a, p. 303) – is, of course, acceptable, provided it is recognized as a mediating process referring to the activity of the brain or some part of that activity. Watson, it may then be said, never intended to reject introspection in this sense. What a lot of trouble we should have been saved if Watson had thought of saying that.

While behaviourists have been returning, in however halting a fashion, to the use of mental concepts, there have been similar trends in philosophy which are highly relevant to the present situation in psychology. The present writer is not competent to give a professional account of these trends, and what follows is to be taken only as a psychologist's attempt to grasp their significance for his subject.

Despite the official separation of psychology and philosophy, they have followed fundamentally the same path. The submergence of the concept of mind in psychology has been paralleled in philosophy by a general rejection of dualism in favour of a behaviourist treatment of mental concepts. There has been a strong tendency to reduce these either to overt behaviour or to dispositions to such behaviour, and the notion that mind might be a reality altogether other than the body was scorned as the myth of the ghost in the machine (Ryle, 1949). But more recently philosophers, like psychologists, have become increasingly aware of the limitations of a behaviourist analysis, and a fresh and still controversial thesis has been proposed, that of mind-brain identity. In one of the earliest statements of this thesis, Place (1956, p. 44) started from a recognition that not all mental concepts could be treated as dispositions to behave in certain ways: 'There would seem to be an intractable residue of concepts,' he wrote, 'clustering round the notions of consciousness, experience, sensation, and mental imagery, where some sort of inner process story is unavoidable.' As we have seen, this is the conclusion to which psychology itself has also been coming.

One might say, to which psychology has been returning, for clearly this marks a recognition that the idea of mental life must after all have some place. This is an extremely interesting development, not least because it inevitably re-opens the whole question of the body-mind relation, which had so long lain dormant. The possibility which immediately springs to mind is that some form of dualism will once again seem appropriate, as in the days when psychology was centred on the study of mental life. Yet any such development would clearly be strongly resisted. The belief that mind and body are radically different challenges the belief that the concepts and methods of the natural sciences are alone acceptable in psychology; and few opinions could be less welcome among psychologists than Stout's view that there was nowhere any place for psychology in the system of the physical sciences. It was to dispose of such beliefs that Watson substituted behaviour for mind, and it is not to be supposed that his successors – even though they are once more talking about mental life – would be pleased to see them back.

Indeed, it is mainly because they have feared such an outcome, that they have so long resisted the return of the repressed. Nor would this outcome be any more welcome, it seems, among many philosophers. As Lewis (1969, p. 205) writes: 'It is assumed that one cannot be philosophically respectable in a scientific age without regarding all reality as somehow capable of scientific investigation.'

It is in this threatening situation that the mind-brain identity thesis comes to the rescue. After stating that some sort of inner process story is unavoidable, Place argues that it does not follow that we are committed to a dualist position 'in which sensations and mental images form a separate category of processes over and above the physical and physiological processes with which they are known to be correlated' (op. cit., p. 44). Instead, 'we can identify consciousness with a given pattern of brain activity' (ibid.). Several versions of this basic thesis have already appeared, but cannot be detailed here (see Borst, 1970). The common aim, however, is to retain the belief that all behaviour is determined by brain activity, but to reconcile this with the recognition that mental states are a real inner cause of behaviour, by postulating that mental states are in fact identical with certain brain states. Armstrong (1965, p. 73) expresses this as follows:

> the verdict of modern science seems to be that the sole cause of mind-betokening behaviour in man and the higher animals is the physicochemical workings of the central nervous system. And so, assuming that we have correctly characterized our concept of mental states as nothing but the cause of certain sorts of behaviour, then we can identify these mental states with purely physical states of the central nervous system.

The relevance of this bold conception to the current situation in psychology is clear enough. The decline of behaviourism has re-opened the whole question of the relation of psychology to physiology. Watson had supposed that the task of psychology was to establish S-R generalizations, leaving to physiology the investigation of the actual neural connections. But, as we saw at the end of the last chapter, the gradual erosion of the S-R formula and the failure of the various indirect methods of identifying inner conditions, has brought us to a position where it seems necessary to introduce physiological mechanisms as an essential part of the explanation of behaviour, rather than as a supplementary study which might be completed later. But this development, it might be argued, brings us back essentially to the situation as it was before Watson formulated his solution. This was the situation, described in Chapter 2, in which James criticized the automaton theory, and in which Stout argued that, if mental processes were mere epiphenomena and only to be explained by connecting them with the brain, then there was no possibility of discovering uniformities among successive mental states, and psychology simply ceased to exist.

The bearing of the identity theory on this problem may be illustrated from a recent exchange of views on the matter. The present writer, in discussing the opinion of some contemporary psychologists that behaviour is to be explained by physiological mechanisms, expressed agreement with Stout (1896) and also Scriven (1964) that this provides a task for the neurophysiologist but leaves no scope for the psychologist (Joynson, 1970). Harré then suggested that the identity theory provided a solution to the difficulty, because 'though a person when looked at from the point of view of his mental functioning presents a very different appearance from how he seems when viewed physiologically, there is one and only one entity involved, as a matter of fact' (Harré, 1971, p. 117). Apparently, the only possible theoretical basis for the explanation of behaviour does lie in the physiology of the brain, but since mental states are to be identified with certain brain states, one may still think of mental states as a real cause of behaviour. (Harré formulated my argument as a dilemma, which I at first accepted as satisfactory (Joynson, 1972); but the comments of Fontana (1972) have convinced me that this formulation is not appropriate, and that the argument should simply centre on the role of physiology in the explanation of behaviour.)

Perhaps it may be suggested that identity theory is just such another half-way house as was epiphenomenalism. The latter doctrine marked the transition from dualism to behaviourism, and gave to mental states no genuine function. Identity theory may be seen as a half-way house on the return journey, and one which again makes mental life superfluous. If one accepts Armstrong's view (1965, p. 73) that 'the sole cause of mind-betokening behaviour ... is the physicochemical workings of the central nervous system', then a knowledge of these workings must be sufficient to account for the behaviour, and further information about the mental states which happen to be identical with certain of the brain states can add nothing essential to the explanation. It is significant that when Harré (1971) attempts to work out the theory more fully in order to illustrate the place of psychological explanation, his account tends to bring out the difference, rather than the identity, of the psychological and the physiological. He postulates three 'tiers' – the first behavioural, the second psychic, and the third physiological. The third is said to 'underwrite' the second, and the second the first. It is not clear what is meant by 'tiers', or how the distinction between the psychic and the physiological tier can be reconciled with the view that they are identical. The relation between these two is said to correspond to that between the physiology of the eye and the gathering of information by looking – which provides an example of the problem, not a solution to it. The introduction of a psychic tier, intermediate between the physiological and the behavioural, seems to have been due to the desire to find a function for mental states, yet this seems to be a move away from identity theory in the direction of dualism. It is not clear why one should not proceed direct from the brain activity to the behaviour via the efferent pathways, or how the psychic tier is supposed to 'underwrite' the behavioural tier. It is difficult to resist the conclusion that the identity theory is a purely verbal solution, which dissolves into what is effectively dualism at any attempt to put it into practice.

Certainly one cannot assume that the identity theory has been established. Borst (1970, p. 29) writes: 'The case for the Identity Theory has not yet been convincingly made out. Some of the logical objections remain inadequately answered; the very intelligibility of the theory is still in dispute; and, of course, its final acceptance must partly await further scientific research.' Lewis (1969, p. 193) writes that

the weight of a very bold theory is made to rest on very scanty evidence and the wishful expectation that it will be confirmed at some future date, in all likelihood a very remote one. A view that is odd almost to the point of paradox ought to have a firmer basis from the start, or at least to be put forward in an extremely tentative fashion.

Nor is it even clear that what Armstrong calls 'the verdict of modern science' would in fact be universally accepted by those in the best position to assess it, for Burt (1968) reviews physiological evidence and opinion, and concludes that a dualistic view is the most appropriate working hypothesis.

A satisfactory approach to the mind-body relation must rest upon physiological and psychological knowledge as well as upon philosophical analysis. Yet one of the most striking features of the identity hypothesis is the dearth of such knowledge : scarcely had it been decided that mental states must after all be admitted, than a solution to the body-mind problem was put forward. But it is a solution which removes the sting of this re-discovery. It enables the theorist to go on talking as if mental life had at last been incorporated in the scientific system, when the actual situation is the reverse. Identity theory has arisen because the behaviourist attempt to treat psychology as a natural science has failed, and the primary object of the theory is to prevent the revival of mental life from disrupting the conventional scientific assumptions. But once it has been re-admitted, it will once again be studied closely, and it may be that the contrast between mental and bodily life will gradually assert itself once more.

There is a remarkable contrast between the position today and that when James's biologist declared that it was high time for scientific men to protest against the recognition of any such thing as consciousness in a scientific investigation. In the nineteenth century such a remark was a daring expression of the revolutionary implications of a science of man. Who could have foreseen that a century later the adherents of physicochemical explanation would themselves be re-admitting the concepts of mental life, and that some would even be urging us to restore consciousness if psychology is not to sink into the limbo? Today it seems that a cycle of thought is rapidly nearing its completion, and that psychology is awakening from its Victorian dream.

The behaviourists naturally like to depict their gradual retreat from Watson's position as if it were an advance. There is a sense, of course, in which it is an advance, for every error which they abandon brings them a little closer to the truth.

G   85

But they must not be allowed to impose the idea that they are exploring uncharted ground. If they could be persuaded to turn round, and look where they are going, they would see that many other psychologists, both past and present, have for a long time been busily engaged in studying the problems of mental life, despite the vigorous efforts of the behaviourists to prevent them. However reluctant he may be to admit it, the behaviourist will have to recognize that he has much to learn from those he has always regarded as outsiders.

We shall shortly return to the contemporary students of mental life, but first we should note that the revival of mental life would be incomplete if it were not accompanied by a re-appraisal of the history of psychology. Under the influence of behaviourism, the earlier period of psychology has suffered an undue neglect. Some writers dismiss the introspective tradition as 'an incredibly flat and barren region of psychology' (Hebb, 1972b). A more discriminating judgment is needed. It has been part of the myth of scientific progress in psychology that the student may be reared on recent experimental papers, and need know little of how his subject has developed. However it may be in the natural sciences, the position in psychology is much more akin to that in philosophy for example, where certain historical writings may be perennially important, not because they embody unchanging truths, but because they explore a point of view which cannot be neglected by those who hope to improve upon it. The neglect of history leads to an illusion of progress through the re-naming of problems, which Allport (1968, p. 33) has described as follows:

> We do not solve our problems. . . . We grow weary of suggestibility and so investigate persuasibility; personality and culture give way to systems theory; the group mind drifts into organizational theory; rationalization becomes cognitive dissonance; friendship masquerades as interpersonal attractiveness; problem-solving dissolves into programming; pleasure and pain become positive and negative reinforcement; maladjustment becomes alienation; volition gives way to decision-making; no longer does one possess character, one has ego-strength. . . . To me such shifting often seems merely weary and evasive – a device for overlooking previously relevant studies.

86

These problems, like so many others in psychology, do not lend themselves to rapid solution through experimental research. This leads only to that 'fragmented, unassimilated hodgepodge' of which the student complains (Deese, 1972, p. 74). The only solution for this state of affairs, it may be suggested, is to place far greater emphasis on systematic reflection and analysis in historically significant work.

By the end of the nineteenth century, the traditional introspective psychology had already travelled a long way towards an enlightened human psychology. Beginning where the layman naturally begins, with a faculty theory, it had subjected this to critical examination, and then explored the more sophisticated theory of associationism. This theory in turn was subjected to radical scrutiny by such writers as James, Ward and Stout, and in their work are to be found the outlines of a subtle and systematic account of human mental life. Passmore (1952, p. xxxviii) writes that 'far from being antiquated, Stout is much more revolutionary than exponents of such "modern" doctrines as the conditioned reflex'. Such judgments may seem far-fetched to a student today, and certainly the contemporary relevance of such writers as Stout cannot be briefly explained; but Passmore's point may be taken as an example. It has often been pointed out that the subsequent theories of behaviourism were to a marked extent a restatement in terms of stimulus and response of the earlier doctrine of association. But Stout was among the most incisive critics of associationism, so that he had in effect already considered much of the substance of behaviourism, and formulated an alternative view, before Watson's version appeared. The fundamental point concerned the 'atomism' of the associationists: they always attempted to explain a given mental whole, or 'frame of mind', by treating it as a mere combination of separate elements or 'ideas'; just as behaviourism was later to be too exclusively concerned with the sheer integration of isolated responses. In contrast to such views, Stout stressed the unity and activity of mind. It was necessary to introduce a distinct kind of mental factor – 'the apprehension of the whole which determines the order and connection of the apprehension of the parts' (Stout, 1896, 2, 41).

From the 'primary fallacy' of atomism, there flowed three 'derivative errors' which prevented the associationists from giving an adequate account of constructive thinking. First, they placed so exclusive an emphasis on mere combination, that they overlooked the importance of the further determination of a whole which in some way already pre-exists. Second, they failed to recognize the apprehension of a *form* of combination as a distinct psychical element. Third, they under-estimated the extent to which elements undergo transformation when they enter a new whole. These views have considerable affinities with the later *Gestalt* criticisms of behaviourism, yet in some ways Stout's views have proved more lasting. For example Stout, unlike *Gestalt* theory, retained a belief in the importance of experience in perception, a belief which has been increasingly vindicated during the last twenty years. It may also be suggested that Stout's treatment of the apprehension of the whole ('noetic synthesis') may still be useful to the modern student of 'creativity' (in his discussion of relative suggestion), and of 'motivation' (in his discussion of conation and cognitive synthesis).

But to suggest that a psychology which is concerned with mental life has much to learn from the introspective tradition, is not to recommend that we should concern ourselves with nothing else. This would run counter to Stout's own conception of the place of the tradition; and since this is a point on which there is a particular danger of being misunderstood, it needs to be especially stressed. As we noted before (in chapter II), the late nineteenth century was a period of empirical exploration, as well as introspective penetration and philosophical skill. It was the age of Ebbinghaus, Wundt, Lloyd Morgan, Galton, Binet, Hughlings Jackson, Ehrenfels and Cattell; as well as the age of Brentano, Bain, and Kulpe. It was an age in which many aspects of human psychology, which are now coming back into fashion, were first taken up and explored. But, as we mentioned before, there was little or no sense of opposition between these new areas and the traditional psychology. That was not something which stood in their way, but something which paved their way. It was, in Stout's phrase, a 'chart of the coast' which could now be more and not less useful because it was no longer the whole of psychology, but only a fragment of it. Thus he mentioned the points of view of physiology, of pathology, of ethnology, and of psycho-physical experiment. Each had its own data, and its own distinct and independent ways of collecting and estimating evidence. The 'time-honoured procedure' of introspection might be a help to these investigators, just as they might be to it.

Today, the variety of approaches is greater still, but instead of forming a family of related inquiries, they too often appear as rival possibilities. But a historical perspective teaches us that no single approach is likely to maintain an exclusive position for very long, for each needs the others to form a coherent whole.

6

THE PSYCHOLOGIST'S TASK

We set out to discover the origins of the general tendency of modern psychology to ignore the layman's understanding. Our search began with the traditional psychology of mental life, which attempted, in however limited a way, to do justice to this feature of human nature. We then traced the increasing dissatisfaction with this conception, as it was found to conflict with the methods and concepts of the natural sciences. The dissatisfaction reached its climax in the behaviourist movement, which finally ejected the concept of mind, and thus marked a profound alteration in the centre of gravity of psychology. Before Watson, psychology was centred on the human mind; after Watson, it became centred on animal behaviour. The layman's understanding was now lost to view.

For a long period, the new standpoint provided for the majority of psychologists a stable and satisfying view of their subject and its prospects. As a biological science, its foundations would be laid in the study of the simpler forms of behaviour, and when these had been mastered, but only then, it would be possible to advance with assurance towards the more complex problems of human behaviour. That this advance would one day come, was not in dispute; the foundations were laid to make this possible, and eventually the attempt would be made. There was always a minority who rejected this biological approach, but it held the allegiance of the 'mainstream' of academic psychology.

It seems that today the centre of gravity of psychology is slowly moving again. Over the past twenty years, there has been a gradually increasing interest in the more complex and the more human, in comparison with the earlier emphasis on the simple and the animal. This is not to suggest that interest in the latter has faded, but that it is pursued less exclusively in academic psychology than it used to be, and that it is more readily seen as providing a starting-point for the exploration of human problems. Experimental psychology is more sympathetic to studies of thinking and concept attainment, as well as to sensory perception; to skills and information-processing, as well as to simple reactions. The whole movement towards embracing 'inner conditions' reflects this same general shift of emphasis. At the same time, there has been a rapid growth of social psychology and personality, which are now among the most popular areas of psychological inquiry; and the academic psychologist is taking a greater interest in the practical applications of his work. All this means that the human being is becoming a much more central figure in psychology than he was before.

The earlier movement, from human mind to animal behaviour, was accompanied by a lively debate on fundamental issues, and eventually led to a radical change in the conception of the psychologist's task. The present movement, back from the simple to the complex, has also provoked a similar debate, which raises once again the whole question of the nature of the psychologist's task. The problems of mental life with which we have been concerned form only part of this debate. It has extended also to more practical issues, and to questions of the values held by psychologists and the general relevance of their discipline. Thus we are brought to the question of what are the implications of the present situation in psychology in relation to the task of psychology.

It will be suggested that we may roughly distinguish three main interpretations of the present situation. These are not three sharply divided schools of thought, but convenient descriptions of certain main possibilities, with actual opinions shading from one to the other, and some opinions, perhaps, falling outside this scheme altogether.

One interpretation is that which is held, I think, by the more confident members of the traditional mainstream. This view, which I shall call the 'progressive mainstream' opinion, is that biological psychology has progressed so far with its foundations, that the concepts and methods which have been developed there may now be extended to begin work on the superstructure of human psychology. The task of the psychologist today is to extend the conventional science of animal behaviour to embrace human behaviour as well. But this optimistic view does not exhaust contemporary opinion, which is also to be found departing from this position in two contrasting directions. In one direction, we remain within the general mainstream position, but move towards those who are less confident that the time is ripe for these extensions, and less satisfied with the progress which they are making. This brings us to what may be called the 'conservative mainstream' opinion, whose more cautious adherents fear that much is to be lost by premature adventures into the complexities of human behaviour, and feel disquiet at many current developments. In another direction, contemporary opinion moves away from the mainstream altogether, towards those who welcome a broadening of the interests of academic psychology, but who deny that its conventional concepts and methods are appropriate, and look for a radical alternative. This position is the successor of that 'minority' opinion which has always opposed the conception of psychology as a biological science. This last position embraces many shades of opinion.

In comparing these three positions, we may begin from an instructive paper by Warr (1973), entitled 'Towards a more human psychology'. Warr reviews current criticisms of academic psychology and suggests that, while the critics naturally vary in their objections and objectives, they share a common theme, namely, 'that academic psychology misses many of the essentially human aspects of life' (Warr, 1973, p. 6). Specifically, psychology has been too exclusively mechanistic, pure, and individual in its orientation; it should give greater weight to the experiential, the applied, and the social. This change is desirable because at present psychology fails to cover its field. It is possible, he writes, because of the 'rapid progress and consolidation we have seen in the last thirty years or so', and because 'conventional procedures and concepts have provided a solid base on which to build – outwards as well as upwards' (ibid.).

This may well be seen as an attractive and moderate proposal, well calculated to heal the breach between academic psychology and its critics. It meets the complaint of the minority that much psychology has been too remote from human interest, and yet at the same time it adheres to 'conventional procedures and concepts'. This view, it may be suggested, belongs to the 'progressive mainstream', and implies that if the 'conservative mainstream' would move forward, the just criticisms of the minority would be met. But we must ask whether this analysis is not too simple and too reassuring.

Warr's analysis overlooks a major factor in the situation. It overlooks the remarkable extent to which mainstream psychology has already begun to move in the general direction in which he points. Experimental psychology has been moving towards more complex problems in human psychology, and during the past twenty years there has been a massive movement by what we called the 'progressive mainstream' to apply 'conventional procedures and concepts' in areas which had previously been regarded as still largely outside their scope. In social psychology, in personality, in child psychology, in educational, clinical and occupational psychology, there has been an extension of these tools on a large scale. Warr is to a large extent preaching to the converted, because the movement for which he calls has already been under way for many years. It is a most striking feature of contemporary psychology that many of the most impeccably behaviourist and experimental psychologists are already working towards 'the more human aspects'. Broadbent is concerned with applied psychology; Skinner applies his theories to language and social problems; Eysenck is a student of personality; J. G. Taylor advocates the restoration of consciousness. Of course it might be urged, especially by the minority, that this movement has a very long way to go; but no analysis of the current situation can be adequate which does not include this central feature.

Moreover it is this feature which has largely precipitated the

93

current debate, because this movement has aroused the opposition of the minority. In earlier times they were left in relative isolation to cultivate their interest in human nature, but now they find themselves invaded by the 'progressive mainstream'. The conventional procedures and concepts are no longer mainly restricted to the simpler forms of behaviour in the original fields of biological psychology, but are increasingly introduced where they rarely appeared before. Thus the most lively and significant of the current arguments have taken place where the frontier of mainstream psychology has been pushed forward, to meet opposition from those who reject its concepts: as when Skinner's views on language meet the criticism of Chomsky; or when Eysenck's advocacy of behaviour therapy is challenged by Bannister. Thus the solution which Warr proposes – the extension of conventional procedures and concepts to the more human aspects of psychology – is to a large extent the cause of the trouble; and its further extension is more likely to promote fresh argument than to reconcile the parties.

But this conclusion, it might be argued, is too favourable to the critical minority who reject conventional procedures. In reality, it might be said, the position is much more promising for mainstream psychology. Perhaps Warr's analysis was incomplete, but the addition which has been made only shows that mainstream psychology is less conservative than Warr supposed. It is in fact already moving outwards from its securely established base, to achieve that mastery of human psychology which was always its ultimate goal. The current opposition comes only from those who have never understood the principles of psychological science, and will soon be overcome. It is a desperate rear-guard action – the last kick of a dying culture – shortly to disappear before the irresistible advance of the science of behaviour.

It is just at this point, when the triumph of mainstream psychology might seem assured, that another factor makes its appearance. For now we seem to have made nonsense of Warr's analysis. How odd it would be if he had chosen the moment when the mainstream was moving successfully forward, its critics finally discredited, to urge that it should begin to move and pay attention to the critics. But of course he is not so foolish. In drawing attention to a feature which he overlooks – the extent to which academic psychology has already moved – we must not give that feature so exclusive a prominence that we allow the truth in Warr's account to be obscured. It remains true that a very substantial body of mainstream opinion is reluctant to move. This transforms the situation. Mainstream psychology does not present a unified body of opinion, but varies from a progressive wing which presses confidently forward to a conservative wing which holds cautiously back. The current debate is not simply a dispute between a 'conservative mainstream' which refuses to move towards a more human psychology, and a minority of critics, as Warr's account suggests (though it does contain this element). Nor is it simply a confrontation between a 'progressive mainstream' which is already on the move, and a minority of critics, which was the next thing we considered (though again it does contain this element). It is really three-cornered, and the 'progressive mainstream' is not merely opposed by the critics, it is also, though less obviously, undermined by the doubts of the 'conservatives'. It remains to consider this last relation.

The programme of mainstream psychology is naturally exposed to a certain tension between what I have called 'conservatives' and 'progressives'. It held originally that the time was not yet ripe for studying the more complex human problems. The fundamental research must first be completed. Much would seem remote from the ultimate concerns of psychology, and irrelevant to pressing human needs. The temptation to deviate would often be strong. But one day, though not perhaps in our lifetime, the basic foundations would be secure, and a psychology sound in both theory and practice would find a not unworthy place among the natural sciences. In the early stages, such a programme raises little difficulty. Energies are concentrated on the foundations, and the distant goal of human understanding serves as the ultimate hope and inspiration. As time passes, the magnitude of the task becomes more obvious, and the need for patience and perseverance becomes more evident. The downhearted must be encouraged with the conviction that the goal is approaching, but they must not be so strongly encouraged that they imagine it is actually at hand. Eventually it requires considerable finesse to maintain a balanced position: as a science, psychology must be old enough to have made reassuring progress, but young enough to explain why it has not made more. At last, a serious division of opinion comes: the more confident press forward; the more cautious hold back.

There was evidence of such a tension in a forcible expression of the mainstream position given by Zangwill (1950) more than twenty years ago. We have already referred, in the first chapter, to his view that scientific study to date had added little that was new to our understanding of personality and social psychology. Similar doubts were expressed about the assessment of intelligence. This was a 'technology whose theoretical foundations are distinctly insecure' and its basic procedures could 'hardly be said to derive from established scientific principles' (ibid., pp. 141-2). But clearly if these major areas of human psychology were so insecure, great caution would be needed with respect to the applications of psychology. This was strongly expressed. Psychology might have much to gain from responding to practical challenges, but (ibid., pp. 213-19)

> real and dangerous problems arise if we accept the contemporary challenge in full measure. . . . We have very few established principles to apply. . . . Psychology *at the present day* is quite incapable of solving the vast majority of human social problems. . . . No immediate practical benefits are to be anticipated from the application of psychological methods to the problems of contemporary society. . . . Bogus science spells disaster.

This position, it will be seen, is not due to inertia or lack of interest, but to a genuine fear of premature attempts to solve problems of great complexity; and is stimulated by a desire to re-assert the need for caution as against those who are over-eager to respond to practical demands. More recently, he has referred with sympathy to those who have thought that there was a 'distinct danger that psychology . . . might generate expectations that it could not fulfil and seek to develop a professional role before its scientific foundations had been securely laid' (Zangwill, 1972, p. 314). That such fears are widespread is suggested by Deese (1972, p. 27) when he writes: 'the attempt to press the whole traditional scientific apparatus into developing areas in psychology induces the very discrepancy between the significance of psychology and the triviality of the problems actually investigated that alarms and distresses students and psychologist alike.' If there was not a strong resistance to these developments, it would be incomprehensible that Warr should feel it necessary to argue in their support, or suggest that changes are desirable with respect to teaching, research, journal policy, and so on (Warr, 1973). The 'progressive mainstream' has to reckon, not only with the critical minority who oppose their advance, but also with the 'conservative mainstream' who undermine their position from behind. Those who agree with Zangwill that 'we have very few established principles to apply', can hardly also agree with Warr that we have 'a solid base on which to build'.

But the movement towards a more human psychology has now acquired too great a momentum to be stopped. Nor is it desirable that it should be. Whether biological psychology has few or many established principles, they are now being put to the test. From the point of view of the critic, this is much the best way in which their limitations can be revealed, and the need for more adequate principles demonstrated. The critic can understand the reluctance of the conservative mainstream to endorse the adventures upon which the progressives have embarked. As we have seen, the method of objective experiment, upon which biological psychology was founded, has broken down : and if it was not even adequate for the simpler forms of behaviour, there is little chance that it will prove effective for the more complex. The critic can therefore take a cheerful view of the outcome. As the contemporary movement progresses, it will seem less and less reasonable to ascribe so exclusive a pre-eminence to the biological standpoint, and as fresh concepts and methods are developed, old assumptions will be abandoned and a new standpoint, centred once more in human psychology, will take its place.

We have suggested that, as the move towards a more human psychology gathers momentum, it will prove necessary to re-consider the aims and methods of psychology. The conception of psychology as the study of behaviour, relying mainly on objective observation, will come to seem a less and less appropriate description of the total field ; and the traditional conception of mental life, using introspective methods, will be given greater weight. But to describe psychology as the study of mind is, for the present writer, at least as much a way of pointing to

97

the kind of problems with which the subject is concerned, as it is of suggesting the kind of solutions which may be found. A more human psychology should mean, at least in the foreseeable future, a more tentative and sceptical psychology; a psychology less certain that it will one day bridge the chasm between its achievements and its goals; a psychology which is always about to confess that no one ever really explains anything. We shall therefore conclude by considering some of the questions which remain to be settled before it is possible to give a satisfactory account of the psychologist's task.

We began with the layman's conviction – his belief that he 'often feels directly why he wants to do certain things'. We suggested that in fact the layman's understanding is both reliable and extensive, at least for the purposes of daily life; and that any attempt to define the aims of psychology should ascribe it a central position. We have also suggested that the traditional psychology of mental life may be seen as an attempt, however halting and ineffective, to come to terms with the layman's conviction; whereas the behaviouristic outlook of modern psychology tends to disparage and neglect it. But we have not so far attempted to set out clearly what we take to be the relation between the layman's understanding and the psychologist's task. This central but puzzling question must now be considered.

The heart of the problem, perhaps crudely expressed, seems to be this: if the layman knows why he behaves as he does, he does not need somebody to tell him. It may be that, in the end, we shall be forced to leave it at that; but meanwhile it presents a challenge to which various reactions are possible. By way of approaching these possibilities, we may study the views of a modern philosopher who places great trust in the knowledge of human nature which is possessed by ordinary good sense. We shall, however, ask whether the way in which this is developed is entirely satisfactory.

In *The Concept of Mind*, Ryle writes as follows (1949, p. 7):

Teachers and examiners, magistrates and critics, historians and novelists, confessors and non-commissioned officers, employers, employees and partners, parents, lovers, friends and enemies, all know well enough how to settle their daily questions about the qualities of character and intellect of the individual with whom they have to do. They can appraise his performances, assess his progress, understand his words and actions, discern his motives and see his jokes. If they go wrong, they know how to correct their mistakes. More, they can deliberately influence the minds of those with whom they deal by criticism, example, teaching, punishment, bribery, mockery and persuasion, and then modify their treatments in the light of the results produced.

He later concludes (ibid., p. 325):

... we find something unplausible in the promise of discoveries yet to be made of the hidden causes of our own actions and reactions. We know quite well what caused the farmer to return from market with his pigs unsold. He found that the prices were lower than he had expected. We know quite well why John Doe scowled and slammed the door. He had been insulted. ... But the actions and reactions which their authors can explain are not in need of an ulterior and disparate kind of explanation.

Many psychologists (and philosophers) have, of course, looked for 'ulterior and disparate' kinds of explanation, and have regarded these as more real and important than our ordinary understanding. Those who propose some version of the S-R formula, or advocate a search for physiological mechanisms, are often led to regard these explanations as providing a properly scientific substitute for the dubious accounts of common sense. If psychoanalysis is taken to imply, as it sometimes is, that unconscious motives are always more important than conscious reasons, it falls into the same category. As against any such interpretations of the psychologist's task, Ryle is surely right to re-assert the layman's claims. Stories about ulterior and disparate kinds of explanation are as much metaphysical as scientific; and, as Stout wrote, 'we are incomparably more assured of the general truth of the system of beliefs implied in our daily dealings with our fellow-men than we can be by any metaphysical theory which conflicts with it' (1931, p. 115).

Ryle is not so unkind, however, as to leave the psychologist without occupation. There are plenty of kinds of behaviour for which ordinary good sense has no ready explanation: feeling tongue-tied in the presence of a certain acquaintance; dreaming a certain dream; addressing a friend by the wrong name, and so on. Similarly, errors of perception or memory may call for explanation. Thus we come to the view that the function of psychology is to deal with cases where our everyday understanding has broken down (op. cit., p. 326):

> The classification and diagnosis of exhibitions of our mental impotences require specialized research methods. The explanation of the exhibitions of our mental competences often requires nothing but ordinary good sense.

Perhaps the psychologist should be grateful for crumbs, but I do not think that this description of his function is likely to satisfy him for very long. Cases where ordinary good sense breaks down in daily life are not, after all, very frequent, as witness the first passage which we quoted from Ryle: and it seems very odd if psychology is not to concern itself with the greater part of human behaviour as it occurs in everyday life. Thus the practical upshot of Ryle's position is that, despite his emphasis on ordinary good sense, he steers the psychologist away from a study of behaviour where it is displayed, just as does the behaviourist who regards it as of little significance. But the problems which Ryle regards as genuinely requiring psychological explanation, though we may certainly admit them, seem altogether too peripheral to provide a satisfying definition of psychology. Thus we are thrown back once more on the central puzzle of the behaviour which the layman already understands, but which the psychologist can hardly omit from his inquiries.

Let us approach the problem by considering Ryle's position more closely. He seems to imply that it is only where ordinary good sense fails, that psychological inquiry is needed; so long as it works well, there is nothing for the psychologist to do. But this, it may be suggested, is to confuse the occasions when an application of psychological knowledge is required, with the sphere of theoretical psychology in general. So long as common sense works well, we do not require help from the expert; but it does not follow that his knowledge can be adequately defined simply in terms of the occasions when we need him. The point is best brought out by considering the analogy of other varieties of knowledge, and the anomalies which would arise if we applied Ryle's argument there too.

In general, the layman only needs the expert when his normal competence fails; but the expert's knowledge is not therefore restricted to these matters. A man may usually be able to start his car, and only call the garage when he fails; but engineering is not confined to the study of mechanical faults. One only calls the doctor when one is ill; but anatomy and physiology are not exclusively concerned with disease. The expert's knowledge covers the normal working of the system, as well as its breakdown; indeed, it is inconceivable that the expert should be able to solve the special difficulties which arise, unless his knowledge of the normal working of the system was superior to that of the layman. In addition, so long as our common sense works, we rarely stop to ask ourselves whether it is complete: one accepts that the light comes on because the switch is depressed, however little one may understand about electrical conduction. In the same way, one might argue, Ryle is accepting our everyday knowledge of human behaviour as final, and then supposing that psychology can be adequately defined in terms of the occasions when that knowledge breaks down. He has pointed to some of the problems with which applied psychology must deal, but this does not provide a satisfactory basis for describing the aims of theoretical psychology.

At the same time, the analogy between psychology and other inquiries is imperfect, because the status of ordinary good sense is not the same. In the natural sciences, the explanations of common sense have no essential connection with the phenomena studied. They do not belong to the nature of the object in question; they have no intrinsic interest for the scientist; and they are usually rapidly superseded as the science progresses. But where human beings are concerned, the capacity for self-understanding is itself a characteristic of the creature studied. Even if the capacity is illusory, still the illusion would be a central feature of human nature. In either case, it is essential to the study of man that we should take into account his own testimony. Our everyday understanding can never be regarded as of secondary interest to the psychologist – something which will inevitably be superseded as his study progresses. Rather, the

layman's conviction expresses, as Kohler contended, a fundamental truth. Thus we are once more thrown back to face the
challenge which the layman's claim presents.

We have encountered two remarkably different attitudes
towards the layman's conviction. The first was that of the
behaviourist, who rejected it as intuitive and unreliable, and
denied that there was anything to show for it. The second is that
which we have just met, which rates ordinary good sense so
highly that it is often taken as final. Such disagreements could
only be resolved by examining our everyday understanding
more closely, and it is this, I suggest, which sets us going in a
direction where a solution might be found. Psychology is the
study of man's self-understanding. This conception of the task
of psychology is certainly not novel, neither is it intended to be.
It is intended to refer to a common feature of many psychological theories, from the mentalistic psychologies of the past to
such contemporary positions as the 'personal construct' theory
of Kelly, whose cardinal quality has been described as 'its
recognition that psychology is man's understanding of his own
understanding' (Bannister and Fransella, 1971, p. 12). The
many representatives of this tradition have certainly interpreted
their task in the most varied ways, but they take a common stand
on the central question. When they are confronted with the
conflict between the layman's conviction that he often feels
directly why he wants to do certain things, and the scientific
psychology of our time in which this plays hardly any explicit
part, they agree with Kohler that they must take sides with the
layman.

To take sides with the layman does not only introduce an
aspect of human nature which has been neglected by theoretical
psychology; it also points to an important difference between
the applications of psychology and those of natural science. In
the sciences, knowledge is applied to the control of phenomena
in a purely external fashion. There is no question of seeking the
co-operation of the objects concerned, for they have no opinions
to be consulted and no powers of self-direction to be invoked.
In psychology, it is otherwise. The psychologist must not be
deceived, by his desire to emulate the scientist, into believing
that he too seeks to comprehend an object which does not
comprehend itself. The psychologist can be of practical value

only in so far as he succeeds in increasing the layman's self-understanding, and only to the extent that he contrives to enlist the layman's self-control.

There remain many acute problems; indeed, it might be said that we have only brought the discussion to the point where the real difficulties begin. We have said little or nothing about the varieties of introspection, about the possibility of using it in conjunction with the experimental method, about the analysis of psychological concepts. Here, however, we shall conclude by considering some of the general implications of this conception of psychology, in relation to the themes with which we have been concerned.

The main reason why the introspective study of mental life was so largely abandoned, was that its practitioners were unable to reach the same level of exact general agreement which had proved possible in the natural sciences. Even when allowance is made for the natural exaggerations of their opponents, it remains true that introspective descriptions of perception or thought varied markedly among different investigators, and were entangled with philosophical questions. But if it was not possible to agree on the facts, there was still less likelihood of agreeing on their interpretation. It was for this reason, therefore, that psychologists – and other social scientists too – turned hopefully to the methods of natural science, redefining their inquiries if necessary to suit this new approach. In this way, it was anticipated, it would prove possible to secure agreement about the facts to be observed, and thus provide a firm basis for a generally acceptable interpretation.

Today, it is doubtful whether this hope is ever likely to be fulfilled. Certainly the difficulties are proving far greater than many of its adherents originally supposed. The method of objective experiment can identify and control its variables only at the cost of confining itself to physical and physiological factors which have already been pre-empted by other sciences; and the subject matter of psychology has eluded its grasp, surviving only as an unintended intrusion which the experimenter is unable to handle. Even its staunchest adherents are now covertly returning to the mental life which they had rejected. With respect to the chief gain which was expected to follow, that of deciding among competing interpretations, it is not unreasonable to suggest (though this would be strongly

disputed) that we are no better off than we were in the
1890s.

In this situation, there is a special significance for the
psychologist in those writers who question whether the sciences
of man can ever reach data which are free of interpretation, or
interpretations which can be scientifically verified. In a paper
entitled 'Interpretation and the sciences of man', Charles
Taylor (1971) argues that there is a sense in which interpretation is essential to explanation in these fields. For these studies
are 'hermeneutical' in the sense that, like an attempt to understand historical record, they are trying to make clear a meaning
which is fragmentary or confused or incomplete. There must at
some point be agreement on at least part of the meaning,
otherwise no message can be conveyed, for there is nothing to
provide a starting-point for interpretation. But it follows that
there is something inescapably circular about the attempt,
since there must be an appeal to a common understanding of
the expressions or language involved. If we reject interpretation
of this kind, we must omit important dimensions of human life;
but if we admit it, we cannot escape the circle of interpretation.

In psychology, this circle of interpretation can be seen in
the way we describe our ordinary experience, in which there is
an interdependence between the description of situations, of the
feelings which they arouse, and of the purposes which we
pursue. To describe a situation as terrifying, entails that we feel
fear, and seek safety; to describe it as attractive, entails that we
feel desire and seek possession. Similarly, if we begin with our
feelings, as shame or jealousy, these must be linked with certain
meaningful situations, and issue in certain kinds of action. It is
impossible to describe the situations, or the behaviour, in a
psychologically meaningful way without referring to the feelings
which link them together. The circle of interpretation may vary
greatly from one person to another. If I like a particular person,
I feel joy when he succeeds and sorrow when he fails; if you dislike him, you feel sorrow when he succeeds and joy when he
fails. Often it is easy to appreciate another's interpretations as
different from one's own; but sometimes, as with the schizo-
phrenic or the man from another culture, it may be very
difficult to make sense of his behaviour. Ultimately 'making
sense' means being able to enter into the system of interpretations and values which the other employs, but one can only

agree on this, if there is to some extent a common acceptance of what makes good sense.

Charles Taylor (1971, p. 51) concludes that the sciences of man possess a number of features which are 'radically shocking and unassimilable to the mainstream of modern science'. One is that agreement on interpretations depends upon a certain shared intuition, and if this is missing we reach a point beyond which rational argument cannot go. If we cannot awaken the same intuitions in the other, we can only agree to differ, for the behaviourist realm of demonstrable certainties is unattainable here. Another is that our interpretations depend upon our self-knowledge, so that to improve them we may need to rid our-selves of illusions, and perhaps even change our way of life. A third is that exact prediction is impossible in the sciences of man. Man is a self-defining animal, such that what he becomes depends on what he chooses to make of himself. We cannot know in advance in what terms man will understand himself in the future. We can only look back and try to understand the terms he has used in the past. The sciences of man are inescapably historical.

There are certain beliefs about human beings which we rarely try to formulate clearly in our daily lives, but which neverthe-less seem to be implicit in the way we treat each other, and which come to the fore if we compare ourselves with inanimate things. We regard ourselves as knowing, feeling and willing creatures, and therefore not as mere bodies, but as mind and body in one. We think we are not wholly determined by factors over which we have no control, but are self-determining and therefore responsible at least in part for our actions and our character. We possess a certain unity and individuality, such that our nature cannot be analysed into elements which lack the quality of the whole. We are aware of moral and aesthetic values, and we believe that we possess a knowledge of ourselves which is, in the last resort, inaccessible to others. To the layman, these beliefs – however crudely expressed – are essential to the notion of a person.

When we turn to the conception of man which is suggested to us by the natural sciences, its most striking feature is its reluctance to recognize any of the characteristics which are so essential to the layman's conception. There is nothing surprising in this. Natural science has arisen in the study of material things, whereas the salient qualities of the person are to be found precisely where he differs from material things. But the consequence is that the scientist shows a strong tendency to deny these qualities; to regard the layman's beliefs as an irrational survival from a pre-scientific age; and to suppose that progress necessarily consists in replacing the layman's convictions with modes of understanding which have proved effective in other spheres. If these modes of understanding can find no place for the cardinal qualities of human nature, this is taken to mean, not that these modes of understanding are inappropriate, but that the qualities are unreal.

These questions will ultimately be decided by the progress of the various sciences of man. So far as the attempt to treat psychology as a natural science is concerned, it seems to me unlikely that the layman will be found to be in serious error.

BIBLIOGRAPHY

ALLPORT, G. W. (1968), *The Person in Psychology: Selected Essays*, Beacon Press, Boston, Mass.

ARMSTRONG, D. M. (1965), 'The nature of mind', in Borst, C. V. (ed.), *The Mind-Brain Identity Theory*, Macmillan, London, 1970.

BANNISTER, D. and FRANSELLA, F. (1971), *Inquiring Man*, Penguin Books, Harmondsworth.

BARTLETT, F. C. (1932), *Remembering*, Cambridge University Press.

BITTERMAN, M. E. (1967), 'Learning in animals', in Helson, H. and Bevan, W. (eds), *Contemporary Approaches to Psychology*, Van Nostrand, Princeton.

BORING, E. G. (1953), 'A history of introspection', *Psychol. Bull.*, 50, pp. 169–89.

BORST, C. V. (ed.) (1970), *The Mind-Brain Identity Theory*, Macmillan, London.

BOYLE, D. G. (1972), 'Michotte's ideas', *Bull. Br. Psychol. Soc.*, 25, pp. 89–91.

BRAND, C. (1971), ' "Hercules" nervous breakdown? An appeal to psychology's pessimists', *Bull. Br. Psychol. Soc.*, 24, pp. 307–15.

BROADBENT, D. E. (1961), *Behaviour*, Eyre & Spottiswoode, London.

BROWN, R. (1965), *Social Psychology*, Free Press, New York.

BURT, C. (1962), 'The concept of consciousness', *Br. J. Psychol.*, 53, pp. 229–42.

BURT, C. (1968), 'Brain and consciousness', *Br. J. Psychol.*, 59, pp. 55–69.

CRONBACH, L. J. (1957), 'The two disciplines of scientific psychology', *Amer. Psychologist*, 12, pp. 671–84.

DEESE, J. (1972), *Psychology as Science and Art*, Harcourt Brace Jovanovich, New York.

EYSENCK, H. J. (1965), *Fact and Fiction in Psychology*, Penguin Books, Harmondsworth.

EYSENCK, H. J. (1966), 'Personality and experimental psychology', *Bull. Br. Psychol. Soc.*, 19, pp. 1–28.

FLEW, A. (1965), 'A rational animal', in Smythies, J. R. (ed.), *Brain and Mind*, Routledge & Kegan Paul, London.

FONTANA, D. (1972), Correspondence, *Bull. Br. Psychol. Soc.*, 25, p. 254.

GALANTER, E. (1966), *Textbook of Elementary Psychology*, Holden-Day, San Francisco.

GAULD, A. (1966), 'Could a machine perceive?', *Br. J. Phil. Sci.*, 17, pp. 44–58.

GAULD, A. and STEPHENSON, G. M. (1967), 'Some experiments relating to Bartlett's theory of remembering', *Br. J. Psychol.*, 58, pp. 39–49.

GIBSON, J. J. (1967), in Boring, E. G. and Lindzey, G. (eds), *A History of Psychology in Autobiography*, vol. 5, Appleton-Century-Crofts, New York.

GREGORY, R. L. (1961), 'The brain as an "engineering" problem', in Thorpe, W. H. and Zangwill, O. L. (eds), *Current Problems in Animal Behaviour*, Cambridge University Press.

HARRÉ, R. (1971), 'Joynson's dilemma', *Bull. Br. Psychol. Soc.*, 24, pp. 115–19.

HEBB, D. O. (1949), *The Organization of Behavior*, John Wiley, New York.

HEBB, D. O. (1960), 'The American Revolution', *Amer. Psychologist*, 15, pp. 735–45.

HEBB, D. O. (1966), *Textbook of Psychology*, 2nd ed., Saunders, London.

HEBB, D. O. (1972a), *Textbook of Psychology*, 3rd ed., Saunders, London.

HEBB, D. O. (1972b), Correspondence, *Bull. Br. Psychol. Soc.*, 25, pp. 251–2.

HULL, C. L. (1943), *Principles of Behavior*, Appleton Century, New York.

HUMPHREY, G. (1949), *On Psychology today* (inaugural lecture), Oxford University Press.

HUMPHREY, G. (1951), *Thinking*, Methuen, London.

HUMPHREY, G. and ARGYLE, M. (eds) (1962), *Social Psychology through Experiment*, Methuen, London.

IRION, A. L. (1959), 'Rote learning', in Koch, S. (ed.), *Psychology: A Study of a Science*, vol. 2, McGraw-Hill, New York.

JAMES, W. (1890), *Principles of Psychology*, vol. 1, Holt, New York.

JAMES, W. (1892), *Psychology: Briefer Course*, Holt, New York.

JOYNSON, R. B. (1970), 'The breakdown of modern psychology', *Bull. Br. Psychol. Soc.*, 23, pp. 261–9.

JOYNSON, R. B. (1971), 'Michotte's experimental methods', *Br. J. Psychol.*, 62, pp. 293–302.

JOYNSON, R. B. (1972), 'The return of mind', *Bull. Br. Psychol. Soc.*, 25, pp. 1–10.

JOYNSON, R. B. and NEWSON, L. J. (1962), 'The perception of shape as a function of inclination', *Br. J. Psychol.*, 53, pp. 1–15.

JUNG, J. (1971), *The Experimenter's Dilemma*, Harper & Row, New York.

KAY, H. (1955), 'Learning and retaining verbal material', *Br. J. Psychol.*, 46, pp. 81–100.

KLING, J. W. and RIGGS, L. A. (1972), *Woodworth and Schlosberg's Experimental Psychology*, Methuen, London.

KOCH, S. (ed.) (1959), *Psychology: A Study of a Science*, vol. 3, McGraw-Hill, New York.

KOCH, S. (1964), 'Psychology and emerging conceptions of knowledge as unitary', in Wann, T. W. (ed.), *Behaviorism and Phenomenology*, University of Chicago Press.

KOHLER, W. (1947), *Gestalt Psychology*, Liveright, New York.

LAWLOR, M. (1967), Publications reviewed, *Br. J. Psychol.*, 58, pp. 477–8.

LEWIS, H. D. (1969), *The Elusive Mind*, Allen & Unwin, London.

LOEVINGER, J. (1951), 'Intelligence', in Helson, H. (ed.), *Theoretical Foundations of Psychology*, Van Nostrand, New York.

MACE, C. A. (1965), 'Causal explanations in psychology', in Banks, C. and Broadhurst, P. L. (eds), *Stephanos: Studies in Psychology: Essays presented to Sir Cyril Burt*, University of London Press.

MICHOTTE, A. (1963), *The Perception of Causality*, Methuen, London.

PASSMORE, J. A. (1952), 'Memoir: George Frederick Stout', in Stout, G. F., *God and Nature*, Cambridge University Press.

PLACE, U. T. (1956), 'Is consciousness a brain process?', *Br. J. Psychol.*, 47, pp. 44–50.

ROSENTHAL, R. (1967), 'Covert communication in the psychological experiment', *Psychol. Bull.*, 67, pp. 356–67.

RYLE, G. (1949), *The Concept of Mind*, Hutchinson, London.

SCRIVEN, M. (1964), 'Views of human nature', in Wann, T. W. (ed.), *Behaviorism and Phenomenology*, University of Chicago Press.

SHERRINGTON, C. (1947), *The Integrative Action of the Nervous System*, Cambridge University Press.

SKINNER, B. F. (1972), *Beyond Freedom and Dignity*, Jonathan Cape, London.

STOUT, G. F. (1896), *Analytic Psychology*, 2 vols, Sonnenschein, London.

STOUT, G. F. (1931), *Mind and Matter*, Cambridge University Press.

TAYLOR, CHARLES (1964), *The Explanation of Behaviour*, Routledge & Kegan Paul, London.

TAYLOR, CHARLES (1971), 'Interpretation and the sciences of man', *Review of Metaphysics*, 25, pp. 3–51.

TAYLOR, J. G. (1971), 'A system built upon noise', *Bull. Br. Psychol. Soc.*, 24, pp. 121–5.

TAYLOR, J. G. (1972), Correspondence, *Bull. Br. Psychol. Soc.*, 25, pp. 252–3.

VERNON, P. E. (1964), *Personality Assessment: a Critical Survey*, Methuen, London.

WARD, J. (1893), ' "Modern" psychology: a reflexion', *Mind*, n.s. ii, pp. 54ff.

WARD, J. (1918), *Psychological Principles*, Cambridge University Press.

WARR, P. (1973), 'Towards a more human psychology', *Bull. Br. Psychol. Soc.*, 26, pp. 1–8.

WATSON, J. B. (1914), *Behavior: an Introduction to Comparative Psychology*, Holt, Rinehart & Winston, New York.

WATSON, J. B. (1924a), *Psychology from the Standpoint of a Behaviorist*, 2nd ed., Lippincott, London.

WATSON, J. B. (1924b), *Behaviorism*, University of Chicago Press.

WEISKRANTZ, L. (1964), 'Neurological studies and animal behaviour', in Summerfield, A. (ed.), *Experimental Psychology*, Br. Med. Bull., 20, pp. 1–82.

WELFORD, A. T. and HOUSSIADAS, L. (eds) (1970), *Contemporary Problems in Perception*, Taylor & Francis, London.

WOODWORTH, R. S. and SCHLOSBERG, H. (1954), *Experimental Psychology*, Holt, New York.

BIBLIOGRAPHY

ZANGWILL, O. L. (1950), *An Introduction to Modern Psychology*, Methuen, London.

ZANGWILL, O. L. (1964a), 'Physiological and experimental psychology', in Cohen, J. (ed.), *Readings in Psychology*, Allen & Unwin, London, 1964.

ZANGWILL, O. L. (1964b), 'Neurological studies and human behaviour', in Summerfield, A. (ed.), *Experimental Psychology, Br. Med. Bull.*, 20, pp. 1–82.

ZANGWILL, O. L. (1967), Article on psychology, in *Chambers Encyclopedia*, revised ed. Pergamon Press, Oxford.

ZANGWILL, O. L. (1971), Correspondence, *Bull. Br. Psychol. Soc.*, 24, pp. 88–9.

ZANGWILL, O. L. (1972), Obituary, *Bull. Br. Psychol. Soc.*, 25, pp. 313–14.

INDEX